Customer Service Training Series

Creating a
Customer-Focused
Culture

I0464490

How Any Company or Individual
Can Create a Brand New Customer
Focused Environment

By

Kimberly Peters

For

The Customer Service
Training Institute

Other Books from
The Customer Service Training Institute

Customer Service Basics

Conflict Resolution Skills

Customer Service Over the Phone

How to Create Customers for Life!

Service Recovery Skills

Enhancing the Customer Experience

How to Interact with All
Type of Customers

Customer Service Training for
Service Technicians

Customer Service Training for
Frontline Personnel

Customer Service Training for
Managers & Supervisors

Customer Service Training for
Call Center Employees

Customer Service Certificate Program

Customer Service Train the Trainer
Program

Contents

Introduction

I'm not one of those people who think that as long as we make a good product or deliver a great service that all our customers will represent one big happy family. The sheer idea that delivering good products and services is all that we need to do in order to have customers flocking to our doors or running to our websites is nonsense. If it were that easy we would have many more successful companies and far fewer bankruptcies and failed businesses.

I have been in customer service for over 45 years and have taught it and written about it over the last 30 years. Throughout that time I have worked for small and large businesses, ran my own business and have a seen almost all there is to see when it comes to customer service. Most important, I have seen a HUGE array of mistakes people and companies often make even though they have the best intentions.

This book is intended for everyone from the CEO or President down to the part-time employee in whatever function they serve within the company. It is also written for anyone who has a career in any size company and for those who are currently in their own business or hope to have their own business one day in the future. While you might say this is an overly broad and ambitious audience, I would counter by saying it is the ONLY audience that this book could be written for because EVERYONE, no matter what function or position is critical to the overall customer satisfaction in the company.

Customer Service is not just an idea or a buzzword you throw around to try and convince your customers that you really have their best interests in mind. Instead, customer service needs to be a culture. It needs to be the underlying driving force behind everything you do and how you go about doing business on a daily basis.

Customer Service is also not something that you turn on when things go wrong or whenever something bad happens. It is not something we wheel out when a customer is unhappy or whenever a letter or complaint is lodged against us. Instead, customer service is something we do to minimize those times when things go wrong and to help create a framework and structure designed to handle and resolve problems before they even reach the customer!

Unfortunately, many companies think that customer service is something that can be dictated. They think that as long as they say that they are a customer focused company or individual that is enough. But the truth is that customer service is something that has to be explained, taught be example and engrained in our brains each and every day.

One of the unique aspects of customer service is that even though the top levels of the company might be hugely committed to customer service and thoroughly support it in the company, the primary effects of great customer service come from the efforts and attitudes of the employees that interact with the customers on a daily basis.

Because of this, even though management buy-in and support are extremely important, it is the attitudes and buy-in of all employees that will often make or break the overall success as far a customer service is concerned. That is why we have written this book with such a wide audience.

If you are a CEO, President or owner of a company, then this book will show you how to implement a customer service focused initiative within your company.

It will show you why this is important, how to go about it and how to bring that message down through the ranks to improve customer service throughout the company.

If you are in management at any level, this book will show you how to effectively teach those in your team the importance of delivering a high level of customer service to each and every customer. You will also learn how to take the commands from upper management and bring them down to your team effectively.

Last, but certainly not least for reasons we previously stated, if you are an employee in any capacity for any kind of company, this book will show you why customer service is so important and why you are being asked to adopt certain attitudes, implement certain procedures or do certain tasks. Sometimes understanding the reasons behind doing something makes it much easier to get behind the task and give it your best.

If you are someone still in school, or new to the workforce, or if you are contemplating getting back into the workforce for some reason, this book will help give you the understanding you need to give your best efforts and perform at your highest level. If you are like most people, that is probably one of your most important goals as well.

Regardless of your position in the company or the career path you may find yourself on, customer service needs to be a part of your efforts and skill sets. These skills are among the most demanded skill sets by recruiters and Human Resource professionals. These skills are also in demand when it comes to promotions and other forms of advancement as well. The better and more well-rounded your skills are, the more demand you will find yourself in and the more secure your career will be.

As for how this book is written, you will find it follows a natural progression from chapter to chapter. But we also understand that people who read these kind of business training publication sometimes have urgent or specific needs and tend to look for information on those needs first. So we have written this book in such a manner that you can start at any point or read chapters in any order you wish.

Because of this, you might see some concepts of information repeated in this book more than once. This was done for two main reasons. First, certain things are repeated because they pertain to more than one area or concept and they are included so those who might have started at that chapter will be able to fully understand the content of that chapter.

The second reason is that some concepts or information is so important that it bears repeating so that you will remember it longer and understand it better. Sometimes there is more than one way to explain something and more than one context or situation that it applies to. So if we are able to explain the same topic or concept in more than one way, we will do that to help you learn faster and better.

As you read this book, there are two things that will help you learn better and retain the information for longer period of time.

The first is to try and take what you have read and apply it to your own company, career or situation. Whenever we make things more relevant and more personal we tend to understand it more fully and for longer period of time. So as you read through this book figure out how to apply what you have learned in your own life and career.

The second thing you might want to try is taking notes as you read. Just the process of reading and then summarizing and writing down what you have read involves more senses and helps retention. When you read and then take notes, you are requiring your brain to not only understand what you read but also requiring it to transform that new knowledge into your own words. Then, as you write it you see it and your brain processes it again.

There is no prize for reading through this book faster than anyone else. Read at your own speed so that you can retain more and retain it longer. If you finish a chapter and you don't really understand it, go back and read it again. This book is not that long and speed should not be a pre-requisite. Results are more important than time.

Take your time, understand what you read and you will get the results you wanted when you first started.

What is a Customer Focused Culture?

It seems today that we hear the words "customer focused" all over the place. Every business is customer focused or "customer-centric" or some other term meant to imply that the business is dedicated to making their customers happy. We see this so often that many of us have become somewhat anesthetized by it. By that I mean that see no longer pay attention to it or attach any kind of meaningful value to the words.

The problem is that most of the time these words are used as marketing ploys to make the business appear better in the eyes of the customer. The words are used to make the customer believe that somehow this particular company has dedicated itself to making the customer happy. Sometimes this is true but many other times it is just words.

When a company is truly customer focused, the company has taken measures and made changes to make every aspect of their business as customer friendly and beneficial to the customer as possible. That means carrying or supplying high quality goods and services as well as having customer friendly rules, policies and processes.

When we talk about a culture, we are talking about a philosophy of doing business. We are not just talking about changing one or two rules or policies but instead we are talking about changing our way of thinking. When we change the way we think, we change the way we approach things. When we change our approach that is when the magic happens. That is when we start to make real and meaningful change.

I have worked at companies where they talked a good game when it came to customer service but many of them thought that was all that was involved. They thought that all they had to do was tell their employees to provide good customer service and everything else would fall in line. Unfortunately, that is not how it works.

A customer focused culture is more than just being nice to customers and providing great products.

Instead, we need to look at being customer focused as a change in attitude. A change in the way we do everything in our company. As an employee, it means changing the way we do EVERYTHING when it comes to how we do our jobs.

A culture also differs from an edict or an order by creating an atmosphere that supports that culture and enables it to grow. It means creating an environment that makes it easier to do the right thing and more difficult to buck the trend and do something another way. A customer focused culture steers everyone towards doing things with the customer in mind.

Today a LOT of businesses focus just on the bottom line. They want to make as much money and profit as they can while spending the least time and money making that profit. That is because their culture is profit driven and not customer driven. That kind of culture leads employees and management to think of the company first and the customer second, or sometimes third of fourth. When that happens, we often do things in such a way that the customer suffers.

For those of you that are old enough to remember, when you used to purchase gas at your local gas station an attendant would run out, pump the gas, check your oil, wash your windows and do all of that with a personal greeting and a smile. That was a customer focused approach to selling gas.

Today, we often pump our own gas, pay a premium price for paying with a credit card and we need to wash our own windows and check our own oil. Plus we do that while paying 10 times more for a gallon of gas than we did in the 1950's or 1960's. During those last several decades, at least in the gas station industry, we become more profit driven and less customer driven.

You could make the same argument for retail stores with their self-checkout lanes which replaced human interaction with a computerized terminal. We can see a gradual reduction in services and benefits along with a reduction in product and service quality as well. All while prices continue to rise.

This can happen for a few different reasons. Some of it is driven by the cost of doing business and remaining competitive in the local marketplace. If other businesses are cutting manpower and services while cutting prices then it might be difficult to get people to come to your store and pay higher prices for better service or more personalized service.

Another reason comes from the "bottom line mentality" that many businesses have these days. They look for ways to cut expenses so that there will be greater profits without having larger or greater sales.

If they can stop washing windows and checking oil they can handle twice as many cars in the same amount of time or even reduce the number of attendants required. If they stop pumping all together and go self –service, they can replace all the attendants with one cashier!

With a customer-focused culture, the focus moves slightly away from profit driven decisions to also factoring in the effect on overall customer service impact. That means that before the gas station went to self-service they would consider how their customers might react to such a change. They would seriously look at the local customer base and the other stations in the area to see if that change might be something that their customers might like. Or, equally important, they might look into whether or not such a change might anger or displease their customers.

We should mention at this point that a customer-focused is not only focused on the customer. Instead the focus is balanced in conjunction with the needs and health of the business itself. This means that even though the needs of the customer are important, the ability of the business to generate profits and remain in business is important as well.

After all, if a company or individual is so customer focused that all decisions are based solely on what is best for the customer, it is possible that the company will lose so much money in the process that the overall health and viability of the company will be placed in jeopardy. If these type of decisions are made too often toe company might eventually run out of resources and be forced to shut its doors. When that happens all customer needs to will cease be served as there will be no one left to help them.

The important thing to understand when it comes to being a customer focused company or individual is that it is important to always balance the needs of the company against the needs of the customer. That means having or developing fair rules and procedures that protect BOTH the company and the customer at the same time. This enables both the customer and the company to survive so that the relationship can continue.

This does not mean that a company should never lose money on a transaction or issue with a customer. Companies often spend more than the original purchase price to resolve a problem or complaint. Usually there is a legal, or very good, reason for doing so and the resolution is agreed to in order to fulfill the warranty or make the customer happy.

But sometimes customer demands might be so extreme that it makes little or no sense to agree to those demands. In those cases a customer focused organization will try and come up with a compromise to help satisfy the customer while protecting the business. An organization that is not customer focused will tend to deny excessive demands and adhere only to what is legally required in that situation.

In the eyes of most customers, the difference between a customer friendly or focused company or organization is huge. Customers notice when they are dismissed out of hand by a company that doesn't care about them. They see when someone is trying to work with them and honestly trying to help. When most customers see this type of attitude they usually calm down and work together with the company to get something resolved.

It is when problems are ignored and when people stand behind company created rules, policies and procedures that customers get angry. That is the very situation that truly customer focused companies do their best to avoid or create. By becoming customer focused we learn how to treat customer's right and how to identify their needs. We learn what is important to them and determine how we can go about changing parts of our business model and individual behavior to make the overall customer experience better for every customer.

Why You Need to
Be Customer Focused

Now that we understand what it means to be customer focused, we now need to understand why becoming customer focused is so important. After all, becoming a customer focused organization or individual and creating a customer focused culture requires resources and effort. To make sure that everyone understands why it is a good idea to dedicate that time and those resources is very important.

It is important to understand why your customers buy your products and services. Sometimes we take our customers for granted and just proceed with the feeling that just offering products and services to your customers is all that you need to do. But that approach and attitude can get you into trouble very fast.

The fact is, unless you produce and market your own unique product for which there is no other similar product that accomplishes the same goal or solves the same problem, your customers are very likely to have options when it comes to where they purchase the products and services they need.

But even if you do have a unique product which has no equivalent available anywhere else, your customers still might not buy your product unless they like your business. So don't get cocky or complacent when it comes to customer service even if you do own a monopoly on a certain product or service.

Think way back to the old days for a moment. Everyone has seen movies of the old west or watched shows like Gunsmoke or The Rifleman. They are still on some cable channels today. In those movies every town had a blacksmith, a bar and a general store. So if you wanted a drink, you went to the one bar. If you needed food or clothes, you went to the one General Store. If your horse needed new shoes, or if you needed some iron work done, you went to the one blacksmith. You had no other options.

In those days customer service wasn't all that important. You could get away with most anything because your customers had no other options. You might not like the General Store but if you wanted food or clothes, you had to go there.

The same with the bar and the blacksmith and the doctor and just about everything else. You could get away with any kind of treatment because you were the only option available to most everyone.

But over time, things have slowly changed.

Fifty years ago towns had multiple stores selling the same products and services. There were several gas stations, supermarkets, doctors, restaurants and drinking establishments. In this kind of environment, consumers had more choices when it came to where to purchase what they needed. Because customers now had options, they could go wherever they felt they received the best treatment and the best overall value.

So now the business faced a "new" problem. That was how they were going to be able to hold on to their existing customers while still attracting new ones. So the basics of customer service and customer focused were born. Businesses soon realized that if they didn't provide a certain level of service that the customer would simply go elsewhere to get that level of service. So they had a choice, lose customers or improve customer service.

But over the past two decades perhaps the single most important and challenging change has taken place. That change has been the internet and online shopping. With the advent of being able to shop online, the consumer now has many more options or alternatives then they ever had before. It just makes sense that the more options a customer has, the more a business will have to offer just to keep their existing customers happy.

This has been a logical progression. From the one store model of the old west to the town environment of multiple stores in the 60's, 70's and 80's, now we no longer have to "settle" for what is available locally or within a certain distance. This has changed consumer behavior far more than anything else over the last 50 years.

Think about it for a moment. Today you can visit 20 stores in less than an hour without having to drive to each one. There is a huge savings of time and no gas or fuel expense. You are not limited to what is in your town or even your state. With the same number of mouse clicks you can purchase from a store down the block or another store 3,000 miles away. It makes little or no difference to the consumer.

So the level of competition every business faces today is very much higher than it ever was before. In the past you had to measure up to a few stores in your general area.

It was easy to know who carried what and who offered which service or consumer benefit. Now you might be going up against 1,000's of online retailers each offering the same type of products.

But before we get all depressed, let's look at the good side of all these changes. Fifty years ago your customer pool consisted on your local town and possibly the surrounding area. Now, with the internet, your customer pool can extend to the entire world! You can sell easily to people out of state and in other countries extremely easily. So along with increased competition comes increased opportunity as well.

Customer Service plays a HUGE part of deciding who people will buy from online. Purchasing online is a largely impersonal experience so a friendly and smart talking salesman isn't going to close sales for you. Instead you have to develop an extremely customer friendly business that people will love and come to trust.

This does not happen overnight either. Consumers often require multiple positive experiences before they commit to a certain vendor. Just one purchase or experience usually is not enough. Even more important, EVERY one of those early experiences must be extremely positive or the customer will search elsewhere for their next purchase!

It has been said that it can take as many as 10 positive experiences to counteract the effects of a single negative experience. So if someone has a bad experience with you or your company, you are going to have to jump through hoops the next 5-10 times (if you even get that chance!) just to get back to where you were before the bad experience!

This is why being customer focused is so critical. Customer focused people and organizations create a way of doing business that is designed to be consumer friendly and free of problems. Care is taken to work out problems and "bugs" in everything before things ever get to the customer. This enables businesses to reduce the number of problems and help create more happy customers.

I guess if there were one phrase I would use to describe a customer focused organization or individual it would be that they were "proactive". That means they look for ways to make things better now instead of waiting for something bad to happen. It means they look at every part of their department, or the entire business for problems. They go through every rule or policy to see if it is customer friendly. They look at various process to make sure they are fair and not overly cumbersome.

They do all of this to find every weak point or every loophole that might result in a negative experience or unhappy customer. They know it is better to isolate problems and fix them now before they ever reach the customer. They want to avoid having to fight like hell to get back to where they were before something bad or negative happened.

That means a lot of time, effort and patience must be used just to get an angry customer back to where they were before the problem happened. After all is said and done, the company has not gained much of anything in the process. They have saved a customer but they wouldn't have placed that customer relationship in jeopardy in the first place if it hadn't been because of a problem.

Being customer focused allows your business to be more responsive to every customer's needs and to create a customer experience that makes every customer feel appreciated and valued. This helps separate your business from the rest of the competition. Your goals should be to transform your business into someplace people WANT to go to purchase what they need. Not someplace they HAVE to go.

It might surprise a few people reading this book but price is usually not the most important factor people think about when they consider where to purchase what they need. They think about convenience, the overall customer experience, selection, service and other things before price comes into play.

In fact, the more expensive the purchase, the more all these other factors come into play. Let's face it, you aren't going to lose sleep over something you purchased for $5 if it goes bad or if you are treated poorly. But if you paid $50 or $500 or $5,000 you will think about after sale support and selection far more on those expensive purchases!

Hopefully by now you see a few of the main reasons why becoming customer focused is so important. But now we are going to tackle a problem that sometimes stands in the way of someone becoming customer focused. It is a roadblock that often appears when someone doesn't think a little bit further down the road.

But now that you know why it is so important to become customer focused we are going to show you why it makes financial sense as well. Even if you are not a bean counter" the next chapter is bound to make you look at customer service in a totally different light.

Why You Cannot Measure the True Cost of Becoming Customer Focused

Even though that should be enough to get any company or individual enough incentive to become customer focused. Let's come up with another reason that will approach the issue from another perspective. Let's talk about financial impact.

Sometimes companies resist the efforts required to become customer focused because it takes resources and money to do so. They see the dollars involved and they don't readily see the return on their investment. But the fact is, it can cost up to 10 times more to get a new customer to walk through the doors than it does to keep an existing one happy!

One problem in becoming customer focused is that it is extremely difficult to place a dollar amount on the savings or increased business we will get from our efforts. Granted we will know when a customer returns after a problem but there are so many other factors that we cannot accurately measure we may never know the extent of any profit or loss that was influenced by any of our customers.

So the result is that many companies will refuse to take action, or not realize the need for it, until it is too late. Without being able to show a specific dollar figure or financial impact on the business caused by customer dissatisfaction, it is sometimes extremely hard to get management to commit to spending money and resources fixing a problem they are not even sure exists.

Part of the reason that you cannot place a definitive figure on customer service related issues is that so much of the impact goes on behind the scenes where management and employees are totally in the dark. Sometimes we are not even aware that a problem exists in the first place. So whatever the cause of that problem might be goes unaddressed and effects customer after customer down the road.

Here are some of the reasons why we often are not aware of the full impact of customer service issues in our business or in our careers:

Customers Never Tell Us

Customers are people just like you and I and some of them just do not like confrontation. So while there will be customers who complain about every little thing and have no problem getting in your face any their problems, there will also be a group of customers who will just walk out never to return.

This is important because when a customer is unhappy with us or our business but never brings the problem to our attention, we never get the opportunity to make things right with that customer. Sometimes all it takes is a small gesture or apology to make everything right. But without knowing that the problem exists, we don't get that opportunity to take any corrective action.

As if that was bad enough, when we are not made aware of the problem, the problem will not be fixed. The longer the root cause of the problem goes unaddressed the more customers are going to be effected by it. Even if it is just a small issue that needs to be corrected unless we know about it, we may never correct even the smallest issue. The result is more angry or upset customers and more customer leaving the business for the competition.

We Are Never Sure of Who the Customer Might Tell

Here is one of the most potentially devastating issues we have to deal with when it comes to customer dissatisfaction. We all know that some customers talk and sometimes that is a great thing. That is why word of mouth advertising is so critical to the growth of all businesses. But the opposite is also true. When a customer is upset or disappointed with the business, they will spread negative comments as well and this can hinder the ability of the business to attract new customers.

Add to this the fact that angry people are far more likely to spread negative comments than happy customers and you have a real problem on your hands. But the hidden danger is that we may never know the true depth of the problem because we never find out how many people the angry customer told about their experience.

Plus, we never know how much business we might have lost due to those comments either. Did the angry customer tell 5 people or 50 or even 500? How many of those people went elsewhere due to those comments? How much did those people spend at your competition? Was it $100, $1,000, $100,000 or perhaps $1,000,000? There is no way to accurately determine what the impact of those comments made by just one angry customer.

Here is a perfect example I encountered during one of my jobs many years ago:

I worked for a relatively large company whose offices were located in an industrial park. When it came lunch time we all usually went to one particular place to get sandwiches or sometimes hot food. The food was OK but the place was convenient and the prices reasonable. In fact, we had them cater all our in-house meetings and seminars.

One day a co-worker of mine got a sandwich and the meat was really tough and fatty. It looked like the end of a cut of meat and it was almost inedible. She went back and asked for a new sandwich from a new cut of meat that was not in the meat case. She was refused and was told that her sandwich was just fine and that she was being picky. She argued but they held fast and she walked out.

She told the rest of us and swore that she would never get food from there again. Sure enough, the next day she drove to another sandwich place about a mile further away and bought a sandwich. The sandwich was amazing! It was larger, tastier, the selection was better and the people very helpful and friendly.

The next day another person went to the new place with her and bought lunch. Eventually most of us transferred to the new place and a month later, when our next meeting took place, we asked the new place if they would cater it for us.

They agreed and now they catered all our meetings and food needs.

Now that original sandwich was about $5 which means it cost them less than $2-3 to make it. I estimated that they lost well over $20,000 worth of food and catering business PER YEAR and all of that went to the new place!

The point I am trying to make is that when they refused to make that new sandwich there was no way they knew that refusing to replace that $5 sandwich would cost them over $20,000 in lost business. Had they known that I am sure their answer would have been different.

Even someone like me, who was part of the office and part of the company has no idea who might have told other people about this as well. Maybe someone had a friend in another company and told them and now that company is using the other place as well? The point is, you never know.

You never know who the customer will tell, you never know how many people the customer will tell, and you will never know how much business was effected by those comments either. But once you are aware that this can all be taking place outside of your knowledge, you begin to see the importance of creating as many happy and satisfied customers as possible.

Never Underestimate Viral Communications

Today with the Internet so full of Social Media sites and ways for people to express themselves, we have a different problem to deal with that did not exist 20 years ago.

Remember when we said that there was a group of customer who are reluctant to get into a confrontation and will just walk out the door without saying anything? Well, a large percentage of those customers, who tend to shy away from a physical or phone confrontation, are more than happy to voice their displeasure through the Internet and Social Media. So that means that bad comments and negative experiences are not only easier to share with one person, they can now be shared by hundred, thousands or possibly millions of people with just a few mouse clicks.

Today someone places a video on YouTube and within 24 hours that video could be seen by millions. People share it and repost it to their lists and the whole thing goes viral. The same exact thing can happen with blog posts and comments made by any of your customers! It is not possible to quantify how much damage will be done by those comments.

But the ease of publishing comments, the ability of those comments to be easily shared and posted to others and the sheer volume of people who are on the Internet every day makes this a potential serious problem for non-customer focused companies.

When it comes to whether or not you feel your company, or yourself needs to become more customer focused, I think we can make a few fairly safe assumptions to help us understand the impact of our efforts.

We can safely assume that any angry or dissatisfied customer is bound to share their experience and post comments about you and your company. The question is not whether they are going to share their dissatisfaction it is a matter of how many people they will reach and how many will pay attention and believe them.

We can also assume that the amount of damage being done to your business is likely to be worse than you might think it is. We always tend to minimize negatives in order to make things appear better than they might really be. But even if you try to be accurate and realistic when it comes to determining damage, figure it is worse than you might think.

We can also safely assume that it is always easier and cheaper to fix problems quickly to minimize the damage done to our customers. So it makes sense to be pro-active and customer focused.

Even though it costs money to do so, it will cost you more to constantly put out fires and salvage relationships than it does to fix problems in the first place.

So never believe that even though you cannot place a specific dollar figure on the damage being done by angry customers, don't think that doesn't mean damage isn't being done. Don't think that the inability to accurately determine the cost to your business doesn't mean those costs do not exist.

You have a choice to make and you need to make that choice right now. You can hide behind numbers and doubts or you can step out from behind the doubt and take action now. Doing that might cost you dollars and resources right now but you will gain a lot more in savings down the road.

As it has been said over and over and over again, "Good customer service does not cost you money, it SAVES you money!"

It's about time we all embrace that and take action now.

Why the Customer

Is NOT Always Right!

Let's take a well-known statement and set the record straight. The phrase "They customer is always right" is false! While most of the time the customer will have valid concerns, comments, demands and complaints, that does NOT mean that the customers is always in the right and those are legitimate demands or comments.

There will be times when customers are so far from right you want to stop and scratch your head and try to determine just how they feel they are justified in speaking what they are speaking. Their demands might be excessive, their actions off the wall and their sense of entitlement might be off the charts!

But that doesn't mean that you don't have to deal with them.

A more accurate statement would be "The customer isn't always right but the customer is always the customer". What that means is that even though the customer might be way off base or totally wrong, you still need to have them remain a customer of yours. So their demands or comment, no matter how unreasonable they might be, still need to be addressed by you.

Customers do not walk into your store or purchase your products and services with the expectation of experiencing a problem or having a bad experience. They expect to get what they paid for and they expect to get it in a certain way and within a certain period of time. If you fail to provide an experience that meets all of those expectations, the result is an angry customer.

When something does go wrong, and it will even in the best companies or with the most sincere and hardest working employee, it is how you respond from that point that will make all the difference in the world in turning around the attitude of that customer. Do the right thing quickly and take care of the customer and you can emerge from that situation in an even stronger position with that customer than you had before. But if you drop the ball or take too long, you can create a very angry customer.

That's where the problems really begin.

You can pretty much figure that the longer it takes for you to resolve a situation, the more it is going to cost you to do so. That is because the more time that elapses the more time the customer has to think about their problem. The more time they have to think about their problem the more serious it becomes in their heads and the angrier they get.

So a problem that might have been resolved easily today might require a major effort and expense if we take a week to address it. The customer demands will get higher and the cost involved in reaching a satisfactory resolution will escalate as well. In some cases, customers can get way out of hand when it comes to what they expect in the form of a resolution.

I have had customers withhold $50,000 from a store because a $10 part came in damaged! I have seen contractors called back time and time again because of outrageous demands and expectations from homeowners. In one job I had I dealt with outrageous demands on a regular basis and some of them were just plain crazy!

This is another reason to be customer focused in the first place. When no problems exist, then your chances of getting hit with outrageous demands or dealing with inflated entitlement issues goes way down. After all, the best way to resolve a problem is to keep it from happening in the first place.

But when things do happen, you need to have policies and procedures in place to resolve the problem quickly. You need to have people trained in what to do, how to respond to problems and have expedited ways of cutting through red tape to reduce delays and get the customers problems resolved.

For example, if it normally takes 4 weeks to deliver a product and the customer has a problem with the product that requires replacement, you should have a process in place to either provide them with a loaner product or get that replacement much faster than 4 weeks. This is important because over that 4 weeks you customer will be getting angrier and angrier and then it will cost much more to resolve the problem.

So how do we take a customer who has inflated expectations or is totally wrong in his views or attitudes and turn him into a satisfied and happy customer? Well, the first thing we need to do is respond quickly and reassure the customer that you are there to help them resolve their problem. You want to position yourself and your company as problem solvers who the customer feels are committed to helping them.

Then we need to figure out what we CAN do to help the customer.

We should not focus on what we cannot do but instead on what we can do. Customer focused organizations get things done. They provide solutions to problems and they do it fast and they are fair throughout the process. They reassure the customer and represent themselves as allies in getting situations resolved.

Even though the demands might be excessive there are things we can do and things that we MUST do. We cannot afford to alienate customers and drive them away. We cannot afford to have angry customers out there spreading nasty comments because you though their demands were excessive.

We must also understand that on some level, the customer feels his or her demands are reasonable. That is their perception and that perception might not be based anywhere in reality, it is still real and legitimate to them and that is what matters.

With every customer, reasonable or not, you have to make a decision as to whether or not we really want to keep that customer as OUR customer. We need to place a value on that customer so we can understand what makes sense when it comes to making that customer happy. Without establishing a value for any particular customer you just cannot make an accurate and informed decision on what should be done. To help us make the right business decisions, let's spend a little time on determining the value of any particular customer.

What is the Real Value of a Customer?

Sometimes it is easier to become customer focused when we more fully understand the true value of a customer. Very often businesses and individuals are unaware of how much a customer is really worth to the business. Since our brains usually attach effort and judgment based on the perceived value of what is at stake, understand the true value of a customer will often help us make smarter and better decisions.

It is frustrating at times when businesses make decisions based on what a customer had just purchased. To assume that a customer is worth only what the total of his or her most recent purchase was is very inaccurate and extremely misleading. The reality is that every customer is really worth much more than their most recent purchase.

There are several components that need to be considered when it comes to ascertaining the value of any particular customer. Here are just a few of the main things we need to consider when calculating a customer's worth:

Past Purchases

Past purchases represent a history of what the customer has purchased from you before. This is an indicator of what the customer is likely to purchase in the future. This is useful in determining the total amount of business you can expect from this customer.

For example, if a customer has spent $1,000 a year with your business in each of the last few years, you can reasonably expect that they will spend that much moving forward. The exception to this might be if you sell or they purchase products that are age specific or situation specific. For example, if you sell kids toys, you would see a fall-off in purchases as their children get older and outgrow the need for toys.

This might be even more useful if you have access to demographics that indicate the lifespan of purchases made by your average customer. If a customer is expected to need your products for a period that averages 5 years and he or she has purchased them for the past 4 years, this could indicate the customer reaching the end of the need for your products.

All of this information will help you get a more accurate grasp on what you can expect from this customer moving forward.

Current Purchases

Despite what most people might think, the amount of their current purchase is one of the least important aspects of their value as a customer. While a very large purchase is better than a small one, one single purchase does not equate to anything close to their real value to the company.

This does not mean that you would treat a customer who just spent $25,000 for a new car the same as you would a customer who spent $2.50 on a loaf of bread. After all, the more money the customer spends with you the more profit you will make from that customer and the more you would like to see that customer remain with your business.

Your level of service that you provide EVERY customer should be appropriate for the type and cost of products that you sell. In other words, if I am selling high priced and premium products, I need to provide a high end and premium customer experience to go along with it. That is because people will expect that from the business where they purchase these high end products.

For example, if I walk into a 99 cent store, I do not expect to receive world class service and I don't expect a fancy and eye catching layout in the store. I also do not expect any kind of sales help with the exception of asking someone if they carry a certain product and where that could be found in the store. I would not expect an explanation of features and benefits or assistance in choosing the perfect product for my needs. The type of store and the price of the products dictates that level of service.

Contrast this to a high end electronics store or furniture store. In these stores we expect the sales force to be helpful in assisting us to choose the right product for our application or needs. We expect a clean and well laid out store with attractive displays. We might expect a showroom with desks and chairs and a nice rest room if we need it. All because we are purchasing expensive and high end products and services.

So let your product cost and position in the market dictate the level of service you provide. You can always provide a higher level of service than customers expect from you but you should never try and provide a lower level of service. That will wind up costing you customers, business and profits.

Future Purchases

There are a lot of products and services that easily lend themselves to future business or repeat purchases. If you sell these types of products your customer service will help you keep customers happy so that they continue to purchase those products in the future from your business and not from your competition.

For example, a supermarket does not earn a ton of money from the sale of a single loaf of bread or one quart of milk. But that small profit multiplies over the course of the year as people come back every week or every few days to purchase another loaf of bread and another quart of milk. If they earn 50 cents from the purchase of a quart of milk and you buy one quart per week, then they have earned not just 50 cents from you but $26 over the course of the year! Add to that the number of years that you are likely to continue to drink milk and that profit from just milk alone could go into the thousands!

But if something should happen where the customer becomes unhappy with your store or your milk that future profit would become in danger of moving to the competition. This can easily happen when an employee feels that this is just 50 cents and if the customer leaves and goes somewhere else what is the big deal.

But if the employee was customer focused and understood that this customer was worth thousands to the business, they might treat the situation a little bit differently.

Add-on Purchases

We also sometimes neglect to figure in the amount of add-on or additional purchases a customer might make when he or she comes in to purchase their main item. Accessory sales and sales of other items can add a LOT to the value of a customer and to their total purchases.

Remember the customer who comes in to purchase that quart of milk? Well, while he is there is might need eggs, bread, butter, cereal and a host of other items that they will but because they are already there and it is convenient. So that 50 cent profit from the milk has multiplied into several times that because of add-on purchases!

This is exactly the business model that car dealers, electronics resellers and the big box stores use to generate huge profits and sales. They use their main products to get people through their front door and then provide accessories and other products at great prices to increase the size of every sale. Think about it for a moment. When was the last time you went to a warehouse club or big box retailer and didn't pick up something else while you were there? That is precisely their business model!

This is important because if they do not come in for that main item, they will not be buying the other products from you either. So whenever we try to figure out the value of the customer we must always factor in the value of any add-on purchases that they are likely to make in conjunction with their primary purchases.

Influenced or Recommended Purchases

This is one of the areas where you have to make an educated guess and where you stand to make the largest error in establishing the true value of any particular customer.

Customers are like our ambassadors into the community. If they like the store they will tell other people about it. They will tell co-workers, family, friends and other people about your business and your products. It is just what most people will do.

If they get a great deal or purchase a really great product, they want to brag about it to someone. They want to let everyone know what they bought and how great it is. And if they purchased it at a really great price or got really fast delivery or something else that they loved, they want to tell everyone. The result is that more people hear about you and your business.

But if they have a bad experience, they will not hesitate to share that with other people as well. In fact, studies have shown that people who have negative experiences will tell many more people about it because they are so angry they want the business to suffer. It makes no difference whether or not you actually did anything wrong or treated the customer poorly or not. It is how they feel about the customer experience they received from you.

But the question is "How many people is this customer going to tell?" Are they going to tell 5, 50, 500, 5000 people? We never know how far that customer will go to relay both a positive or negative experience.

For example, if I were to receive a really bad experience from a business, they would have no idea that I give classes in customer service and could use that experience, and their business name in my presentation. So that message might influence thousands of people when it comes to where they purchase. Remember the previous example of the sandwich shop? One bad experience cost that business a ton of money.

Never go under the assumption that this customer doesn't know anyone who can effect your business. Because everyone has friends and relatives and they talk to others as well. You never know how and where their story will spread. I always advise to make your guestimate on the very high side so you won't get blindsided by making the wrong decision.

Even then you might seriously underestimate the wrong customer.

Affiliated Purchases

Sometimes individual customers have associations and relationships you are not aware of that can have a significant impact on you and your business. That is because these relationships and affiliations could wind up costing you business as well. So it is just not the purchases made by the customer that matter but the purchases made by other customers and companies that know your customer.

Let's refer to that sandwich shop again. In that story the old sandwich shop not only lost the business of that customer but they also lost the business of their friends as well (influenced sales). But in that example they also lost the company catering business as well because the food at the new place was better and possibly cheaper.

Almost every customer works for a company is some form. If that company uses your services or purchases your products, that business might be at risk as well if your customer has a poor or negative experience.

The problem with this is that we usually never become aware of who the customer works for or who the customer has a relationship or association with. If you anger or frustrate your customer is he or she going to tell the company he works for, the organizations he is active in and other groups about his experience? It is likely they will especially if they feel they have been treat unfairly.

As you can easily see, there is much more to the value of a customer than the amount of their most recent purchase. Now that you are aware of this, we must do two things.

First, we must educate EVERYONE in the group or company about how to look at the actual value of every customer. We need to make employees and management aware that the person standing before us, or who we are talking to on the phone, might represent a lot more business than we originally thought.

Second, we need to train people to get in the right mindset to where they based their actions and decisions based on the perceived value of that customer. This is important because we tend to treat people differently based on their perceived worth.

Just like the employee who felt that losing the customer who just purchased a quart of milk was no big deal because the business only lost 50 cents, if our employees think that our customers are worth a lot less than they really are they will not give their best effort in helping them and making them happy.

If you have any doubt about how people react to other based on value, think about how you would react if someone offered to pay you $5 for completing a task and another person offered you $50 or $500 to complete the same task. Which one would you give the most effort on? The one that paid $5 or the one who would pay you $500?

You would give the most attention and the highest effort to the one for $500 because your mind would attach more value to that offer as opposed to the other one. This doesn't mean you don't get a benefit from both but that one is more valuable than the other.

A customer focused organization understands that values that their customers represent. They react according to this value and takes the steps necessary to protect the relationship they have with each of their customers. When problems do arise, as they always will, they make their decisions based on the true value of the customer not on just their most recent purchase.

Only when an organization does business and takes action based on these principles can they provide the proper level of service to each and every customer.

What Customers Really Want!

One of the most difficult parts of operating a business is understanding the needs of the customer. Sometimes this is easy but in some businesses in certain industries the real needs of the customer are more difficult to uncover. This is not because the customers are intentionally keeping their needs from the business but that they are just poor communicators. Sometimes even the customers are not aware of what they are really looking for! This might be hard to believe but trust me when I tell you that you will encounter this particular problem many times when dealing with customer problems.

Though every customer is different and also understanding that every situation might be different as well, there is no "one size fits all" approach to customer service and problem resolution.

That being said, there are a few assumptions or generalizations we can use to help us get to the real problems and needs of the customer.

Here are just a few of the most common assumptions we can use to help us correctly identify customer needs:

Customers Are People Just Like Us

With rare exceptions, your customer is likely to be someone pretty much like you and I. These are people with friends and family like you and I and they are people who pretty much use the same criteria when it comes to what we purchase and how we purchase it. Like the old saying goes "We all put our pants on one leg at a time!"

It is important that we understand this because it helps us figure out what the customer is feeling, why they are feeling that way and most important, how they might react to what we are going to say and how we are going to say it.

Though people do differ from one another, it does stand to reason that if you have a certain reaction to something when it is said to you that many customers will have the same reaction.

So if you can honestly say that you believe in what you are saying and truly believe that it is a fair and reasonable response, the customer will as well. Of course, the opposite is true as well.

Customers Generally Want What We Want

If you feel that a policy or rule is not fair to customers there is a good chance the customers are going to feel the same way. The same with what you are going to tell the customer. If your company or manager wants you to say something to the customer and you feel that you would not like to hear that said to you, it is a good bet the customer will not like it either.

All of this means that as a fellow "customer" with pretty much the same needs and feelings of your customer that you will be a pretty good judge of how your customer is going to react. So be honest when you are evaluating a particular resolution before you propose it to the customer. If you feel it is fair, there is a good chance they will feel the same way.

But if you think it is not a good resolution, then try and figure out something better before speaking to the customer. Take it back to your supervisor or manager and nicely state your feelings and concerns. Sometimes you only get one chance to come up with a good resolution and you want to make sure you lead with your best up front.

Otherwise you risk further alienating the customer and making it more difficult and more expensive to resolve the situation moving forward.

Customers are Looking for Solutions
Not Answers

One common misconception is that customers are looking for answers to their problems. This is just not true! What customers are really looking for is a solution to their problem not just an answer. There is a distinct difference.

An answer can be something the customer doesn't want to hear or something that doesn't help him solve his problem. If you fail to deliver a product or replacement part to a homeowner when promised an "answer" might be that you forgot to order it or that it arrived broken is an answer but it is not a solution. Answers do not always make customers happy.

A "solution" is different. A solution gives the customer a resolution to his problem. If you failed to order a part like you said, or if it came in damaged, your "solution" to the homeowner might be to call him and let him know that you ordered a replacement and requested it be sent overnight so the customer will have it the next day. That is much more than an answer, it is a solution.

Despite what you might think, the vast majority of customers do not expect perfection. They understand that mistakes do happen and that no one is perfect. But it is what happens after the mistake that is important. If you take ownership of the problem and take steps to resolve it, that will reassure most customers. But if you just admit the mistake but do not resolve it properly, the customer is likely to remain upset.

Here is what I always felt was the perfect example:

I worked for a company that took approx. 2 weeks to get in parts and products to the customers from the date of the order. But when something went wrong, or when an order was lost or damaged, they just placed a second order and made the customer wait another two weeks. For those customers this often meant waiting a month or more to get what they needed! Needless to say this did not go over well when problems did arise.

A customer focused company would have a process in place where the second order would be placed immediately and expedited so they could have that part or product within a few days instead of two weeks. In those cases the customer would still not be thrilled with the added delay but would still see that the company took ownership and was trying to resolve the situation to the best of their ability.

That is what most customers are looking for. Not perfection but just someone who is trying to do the right thing for the customer.

Sometimes people are angry not so much because a product failed or a deadline hasn't been met that they create demands for things they think they are looking for. For example, if you were supposed to get a customer a replacement part or product by a certain date and you failed to get it to them, they might yell and scream and demand you have it overnighted.

But the fact is they are not made that the part didn't arrive on time, they are upset that they cannot use that part or product to solve a particular need or problem they currently have. If they need a part for their dishwasher and it didn't arrive, they are mad because they will have to hand wash their dishes for another week or two. If their new sound system came in damaged they are not mad that it was damaged, they are mad that they will not be able to use it for their big party this coming weekend!

But if we understand the need behind the demand, perhaps there is another solution that would make the customer happy until the replacement came in. Maybe a loaner sound system could be provided for the big party. Maybe you could work out a discount on another model of dishwasher or off the customer a gift certificate for a local restaurant for a meal or two until the part came in so they wouldn't have those dirty dishes!

You might not think of either resolution if you never stop to think about what this problem really means to this customer! Don't concentrate so much on what the situation is at this point. Instead, think about what problems it has created for the customer and what you might be able to do to solve those immediate problems.

Once we determine what is really impacting the customer and causing them to become upset the faster and better we will be able to come up with a plan to solve their problems and end their frustration. Not only will the customer get their problems solved faster, they will appreciate you and your company making the extra effort and going the extra mile to help them with their problems.

Customers Want to Feel Valued and Appreciated

Here is another way that customer focused organizations and individual employees can make a dramatic impact on customer satisfaction and problem resolution. They can accomplish this by simply realizing and understanding that all customers want and need to feel appreciated, valued and needed. These are basic human emotions that are extremely important to most of us, customers included.

Customer Focused organizations treat the customer like a real person instead of an account number or order number. They thank the customers for their business, take their problems to heart and reassure them that they are there to help them resolve their problems. They do not supply excuses or just answers, they supply solutions.

The amazing thing about this approach is two-fold. First, it costs extremely little in terms of time and resources to convey your appreciation to the customer. It takes just a few seconds to thank them for their business and a few more seconds to let them know you are there to help them. So the cost is extremely minimal and the potential benefits are unlimited. It is so easy every individual and every company should be doing this.

The second thins that is amazing, even downright astounding, are the number of people and companies that are NOT doing this! There are so many people out there continuing to hide behind arbitrary rules and policies and excuses all designed to make things harder for the consumer. To these companies customers are just numbers and policies. They are impersonal and uncaring. And that attitude will factor heavily into how their customers feel about them.

Here is a perfect example of what I am talking about. This happened to me a short while ago and it still frustrates me to this very day.

I purchased a protection plan on some outdoor furniture from what supposedly was a reputable company. I will not give you the name for obvious reasons but here is what I encountered when trying to file a claim:

I was told I would have to fill out forms and physically mail them. I could not do it online or over the phone. This should have been my first warning about what lies ahead!

I received the forms 3 days later and the forms had to be filled out and pictures enclosed and the entire package had to be returned within 10 days of when the forms were requested! This should have been my second warning shot! 3 days had already expired and it would take at least 3 more days for the forms to make it back to the company which means I had, at the most, four days to fill out these forms! Had I been on vacation or sick, I was out of luck.

I filled out the forms and sent them back. I heard nothing for over a month. I called back and was told they never received the forms. So I had to go through the whole process again. The forms were sent to a Post Office box so you could not get a signature for delivery. (Third warning sign!)

By this time it was too cold to do the service so I asked if the service could be postponed until after winter was over. I was assured that it could. But when I called in the spring I was told the service time frame had expired and I would have to start all over again.

So I submitted all the forms and received a notice a month later telling me that I did not schedule service in time so my claim was being denied. When I called, after 18 months of nonsense, I was them told my particular problem was not covered under the protection plan!

As you can imagine, I was livid not only at the delays, but the arbitrary policies that were put in place by the company to protect their interests and not mine. That 10 days policy should have been at least 30 days to be fair to the customer.

I left this experience with the feeling that this particular company cared nothing at all about me the customer and after reading comments on their website I was convinced as there were numerous other comments from people experiencing the same problem and getting the same treatment.

Needless to say I went back to where I bought the furniture and complained to them but I would likely never purchase anything from that company again. I will also likely do whatever I can (within the guidelines of the law) to make sure others do not fall victim to what I had happen to me.

Customers are Looking for Empathy

In the previous example, which I apologize for being so lengthy, you also saw that this company has zero empathy for my situation. No one ever acted like they gave a hoot about what I was going through. No one stood up and did anything to circumvent the system or get service out to my home to resolve the problem. Instead they stood behind their rules and [polices to protect their own corporate interests.

Customers need someone to at least convey their understanding. They want someone to say they are sorry that you are in that particular situation and that they will do their best to get it resolved. This is NOT about accepting blame, this is about trying to get to the bottom of the problem and give the customer a resolution or at least a direction on what needs to happen next.

In the example we just read you will see that there were at least 4 or 5 conversations with a representative and none of those people told me that my problem wasn't covered.

If they had I could have taken other steps 2 years ago to resolve the issue direct with the manufacturer. But the representatives were so focused on following their rules and procedures and denying service they failed to even take a look at what the problem was that was being reported!

The right thing to do would have been to tell me that my problem was not covered and to direct me back to the manufacturer who had their own warranty on the furniture. Had they done that I could have received service from the manufacturer and my problem would have been resolved. But since everything had to go through this company first, nothing happened for almost two year!

As we have said a few times already, the vast majority of customers do not expect perfection or to have every demand agreed to and handled yesterday. But they do expect to speak to people who at least say they are committed to helping and they need to feel appreciated and valued as a customer of the company. When that doesn't happen things usually go rapidly downhill very quickly.

If I were to sum up customer expectations in a very simple way, I would say that customers expect to be treated fairly, be made to feel wanted and appreciated and expect to either have their problem resolved or be closer to that goal at the end of the conversation or encounter. If you and your company can accomplish by becoming more customer focused, then your business will create more loyal customers now and in the future.

The Need to Be Pro-Active

Hopefully by this point we have given you enough information and background to get your buy-in on becoming a customer focused organization or individual. But just in case you are still not convinced, let's discuss one more important reason for every company or individual to adopt a customer focused mindset.

Being customer-focused means changing the way everyone is thinking so that every decision, every policy and every rule has portions of it that are customer friendly. That means that every part of the way we do business not only protects the interests of the company but the interests of the customer as well.

This is an important focus because it gets everyone thinking about the customer and what impacts them on a daily basis.

It causes us to look at things through the customer's eyes and not just as it is seen by the business. When we do this we then have the ability to see things in a different light and uncover certain issues or problems that otherwise might have gone undiscovered.

We all need to agree that there will be problems no matter how careful we are and how dedicated we might be. Things will always find cracks to fall through and people will always have distractions that keep them from doing what they should be doing and doing so in a timely manner. In other words, even in the best and most dedicated companies and the most dedicated employees, stuff happens.

But it is not those problems that should concern us all that much because we really cannot possibly control the things that can go wrong for a myriad of reasons. Instead, we need to get our hands around the things we can control and the problems we can identify and do our best to work on those things so that they cease to cause problems for our customers.

I'm sure we all can agree that the earlier we identify and solve a problem, the better our business and our customers will be. Identifying and resolving issues fast means that fewer are impacted and the overall impact to the company and the customer is very limited. While that is a worthy enough goal for most companies, we want to set our sights on a goal just a little bit higher.

We want to stop problems before they actually become problems.

Now you might be asking yourself right now how you can possibly solve something before it happens. While most of us have tools that will help us do our jobs better and serve our customers better, most of us do not possess anything like a crystal ball that can accurately predict the future. Since that is the case, what do you think might be the best thing we can do to resolve problems before they get started?

We need to become more pro-active. And that means actively searching out for inadequacies and issues that currently exist that have the ability to impact customers negatively in the future. Then, once these issues have been identified, they are addressed before they come in contact with any customers in the future.

Now all of this sounds great but how exactly does a customer focused organization or individual accomplish this? Well, the answer to that is surprisingly simple. We just have to start putting ourselves in the position of the customer and start going over our entire business or department piece by piece from a customer point of view. You might be shocked to see the potential issues that are easily identified once you look at some things from the customer point of view.

Let's look at a few examples that can illustrate what we are saying:

When we look at our return policy we see that all returns are subject to a 10 day limit. After 10 days a 25% restocking fee will be charged. Now this was put into place to protect the business and recoup the cost of manually accepting returns, adjust inventory, restocking them and other misc. processes. It protects the company but from the customer point of view the time frame is too short and the restocking fee might be too high.

A customer focused employee might look at this policy as being customer unfriendly because of the short window of opportunity. So they might suggest 30 days instead of 10 days so that vacations and other obligations or situations do not unfairly penalize the customer. That would make the policy a lot more appealing to the customer.

Second, a customer focused company would look around at the competition to see what other companies are doing regarding returns and see if they are charging similar fees. If no one else is charging them then a good argument should be made for eliminating the fees in your company. Failure to do that might lead your customers to start purchasing at stores that do not charge those fees. If research finds fees are charged at other similar companies then you might consider lowering the fees to make them impact the customers less.

The same might apply to delivery scheduling. Let's say you have a policy that you do not give specific delivery times. You just give a date when the product will be delivered. While that makes scheduling deliveries easier for you it also requires a customer to arrange to be home for the whole day instead of just a morning or afternoon. Maybe they have to take a full day off of work instead of just a few hours.

That is easier and friendlier for the company and those who schedule deliveries and load the trucks but it is not at all customer friendly. When you look at it from a customer point of view you might change your policy to give a half day window, say morning or afternoon, as a time frame. Even better, maybe you can give a two hour window so that people might be able to utilize a bigger part of their day.

Think about how a customer might feel if they took a full day off of work only to have their delivery done at 8:10 AM. While some customers might be thrilled to have the rest of the day to do whatever they wanted, a segment of the customers would be angry that they had to take a full day off. So the narrower the time frame the better it is for the customers.

You can make the same argument for every rule, policy and guideline that you have in your job or your company. Therefore you need to take EVERY one of those rules and guidelines and go through them from a customer perspective. Be brutally honest with yourself and write down everything that a customer might object to. You will not have to change everything but what you can change will help you become more customer friendly.

As we go through this exercise I want to say again that while we look at things from the customer's perspective we must also keep the interests of the business in mind as well. Because of this certain things will be able to be changed while others should not. There will be compromising to be done in an attempt to meet the customer halfway whenever possible.

The whole goal here is to look at EVERY aspect of the business to see how customer friendly / unfriendly any part might be. Then, we can make efforts to create a much better overall customer experience.

By doing this we can get some insight into what might possibly cause problems or issues in the future. We can take cumbersome processes and streamline them. We can take policies that favor the business far too much and make them more fair and lenient in the eyes of the customer. We can make every part of our business more responsive to the needs of the customers.

Another benefit of being pro-active is that we can also improve on areas that might not need improvement right now but could still be made better. Since our end goal should not just be to meet a customer's expectations but to exceed them, making something that is already good into something that is great is what could separate you from everyone else.

And that brings us to another aspect of being pro-active.

Many business start out as extremely customer focused but then become complacent thinking and believing that they are still the best. But the problem is that over time as other businesses see what you are doing and copy your strong points they move further ahead of you as they improve while you sit there patting yourself on the back.

So the result is that you and your business by doing nothing actually fall further behind. Pro-active businesses, on the other hand, are ALWAYS looking for something that can be made better. They search the competition and copy what others are doing and placing their own spin on it to make their business even better.

They do not wait until they HAVE to improve, they improve before others recognize the need for improvement.

The best businesses look for ways to improve EVERY ASPECT of their business. Then they make improvements and implement them. Then they look for ways to improve further and they keep replaying that same cycle over and over and over again until they have exhausted all ideas and all possibilities. Even then, they look for new and unconventional ways of making their business bigger and better.

The alternative is to constantly spend time and resources putting out fires and trying to win back angry and disappointed customers.

The alternative is to continually lose customers to your competition because of problems you don't know exist because you never took the time to investigate or analyze them.

The alternative is to develop a reputation of a business that is not customer friendly and to have to fight other businesses with better reputation and a better track record.

Last, but certainly not least, is that the alternative is having to fight back so much and spend so much in time and resources that your business might never recover because you have waited too long and caused too many problems for your customers.

I'm sure we all can agree that adopting a pro-active approach is much more efficient and much smarter than any or all of these alternatives.

Products, Services & Customer Service

Over the course of my career, I have seen a LOT of different things that have had both positive and negative impacts upon customer service. But contrary to what may people might think not everything revolves around policies, procedures and the people who apply them. There are other factors involved as well.

Products and the services we provide play a HUGE role in how our customer service is perceived by our customers. We can have the best and most dedicated people in the world interact with our customers but if our products and services are crap not else stands a chance of being successful.

As we have said before, reasonable customers do not expect perfection. Instead they want a reasonable level of expectation that their experience will be relatively problem free but when a problem does occur that you will deal with it quickly and effectively. In other words, they expect things to go right but if they don't, they expect you to fix it.

It also has been said that companies can use problems to show customers just how good they are and come out of a negative situation with a customer for life. This can definitely happen and there are hundreds of cases where this has occurred. After all nothing shows how customer focused you really are than demonstrating it by taking a customer problems and resolving it on the spot.

But that only works when you resolve a problem and that problem is not followed up by another problem and another problem after that. In order to make customers happy you have to give them good products that do what they are marketed to do and when they don't you must take swift and positive action to resolve the issue immediately.

If I buy a product and it breaks down but you air overnight a replacement, chances are I will be happy with your efforts. But if the new one breaks down as well, that is not good for the product or the company that sold it. If you provide a service and the service is done poorly, doing the job over again will only be successful if the second time is done perfectly.

It is amazing how many companies fail to grasp this extremely basic and simple concept. Despite common sense, there are people out there who honestly believe that customers should be happy with products that are of low quality or have frequent problems. I know this from experience.

I worked for one of the most respected and well known companies in one industry for many years. We had a solid reputation for quality and took pride in our product and in our service to our customers. In the beginning almost all our efforts were focused on making quality products and then going over and above when the rare problem occurred. Our unwritten rule was that if a customer did an issue, you did what had to be done to resolve it and at no charge to the customer.

Then, over the years management was brought in from outside the company and with those changes came a different corporate attitude and focus. We now became more focused on sales and profits and offering more product. We paid workers less in salary and benefits while at the same time increased the bonuses of the upper management.

Quality suffered, service increased, problems increased and customer began to complain and question our products.

It was obvious to everyone why things were the way they were but we were stunned when we found out how management expected us to deal with this situation.

Instead of improving quality and changing policies and procedure to insure higher quality, we instead were told that it was up to us to "reset" the expectations of the customers! Yes, you read that right. We were expected to go out and tell the customer in a nice way that they really had no right to expect to get a quality product and that they should be happy to settle for something less than what they purchased.

Needless to say, that did not go over well.

So if you are a CEO or manager in a company, or even if you own your own small business, let me give you one clear and important fact right here and now. That fact is, if you do not produce quality products and services, no amount of after sale customer support or customer focus is going to help you keep your customers.

You cannot dictate to a customer what their expectations should be. A customer expects what he expects whether those expectations are right or wrong. You can attempt to educate them and set them straight as far as what is reasonable and correct any misunderstandings but you cannot go out and make someone happy by just telling them their expectations are too high!

It just doesn't work. You cannot dictate customer service and you cannot dictate a customer's expectations.

The customer service experience starts with how the product is marketed and represented by the sales force at the dealer. Hopefully the salesman and marketing materials are honest and straightforward and accurately describe what the product or service can do and how it is designed to be used. If you are relying on deceptive or overly aggressive marketing or sale techniques, your troubles can start right here.

From this point onward, your products and services are going to be the primary factor in contributing to how your company and its employees are regarded in the industry. If you produce a quality product that functions like it was marketed with very limited problems, your future customer service wise will be bright as long as you have the right people and policies in place.

But if your product does not do what you claimed in would, or if the quality is so poor that you cannot keep it operational, then your customer service is going to take a huge hit. There are no words that can make an angry customer become happy with a product that doesn't work or is not reliable.

Great customer service will help you resolve problems satisfactorily only when those problems are replaced with new ones.

Great customer service cannot make up for shoddy products or deceptive marketing.

Great customer service will not be enough to allow you to rest a customer's expectation down to a lower level just because you want them at that level.

To summarize what we are saying, you cannot just make a statement that customers should be happy with your company and expect that to come true. You cannot dictate to employees that it is their responsibility to make customer satisfaction go higher when your products are of inferior quality.

Customers will only be happy when they purchase products that work and get quality help when they don't work. Even then, once a customer has a problem it had better be a long time before they experience another problem or that could very well be the last time you sell the product to that customer again.

The Trickle-Down Culture

Now that we are all on the same page and understand why we should be customer-focused and have had a myth or two exposed along the way, we come to the part where we discuss how to develop a first class customer focused organization. In other words, this is where we either put up or shut up. So with all that in mind, let's start from the top down.

As we have already said, being customer focused is a culture and an attitude not an order or demand. The message needs to start at the top and be gradually brought down through the entire organization. Plus, as the messages brought down, the entire business structure and policies must be aligned so that they support and help nurture this new attitude and approach to customer service.

There cannot and should not be mixed message from upper management where you are told one thing and asked to do another. For example, you cannot be told to increase manpower so customers do not have to wait as long as they currently are but then cut manpower budgets to make that impossible.

You cannot expect to train an entire company on customer service or anything else but not give them the budget or resources in which to do that. Though this might sound very basic, this very attitude is something that I have run into several times throughout my career.

I have been tasked with getting a staff trained but given no funds to hire trainers or even get training materials.

I have been asked to dedicated personnel to improve customer service but not allowed to hire the people to do so.

To take things to an even more absurd level, at one job I was responsible for controlling the number of service calls that were generating by our products. The fact that no one inside the company had any influence at all on whether or not someone called in with a service request made no difference at all.

The fact that the ONLY thing we could do to reduce service volume was to improve quality or sell less product was lost on management.

For those who might be curious, this was the same management team who said that we needed to rest our customer's expectations!

Once a company decides to become customer focused, that commitment must start from the top and move downward. Everything that comes down from up top must be customer focused and customer smart. Every decision must be made with taking the customer into consideration. While balance is important, we cannot create and enforce one sided policies while expecting employees to focus more on the customers.

It is also a fallacy that customer service is only confined to those employees who deal with the customers on a regular basis. The reality is that EVERYONE and EVERY PART of the company needs to be customer focused in order for the company to be successful!

That means everyone needs to have the same goals and focus. That means every employee and every manager in every department must do what they can to improve the company and become more customer focused. It all starts from the top and works its way downward. It cannot work the other way or just start from the middle down.

That means that management must understand the need to work on every part of the customer experience and all the people and processes that make up that experience. Management must understand that the entire customer experience is much like a chain and if any one link should fail the entire experience will fall apart.

A great salesman might close a huge sale but if they do that by misrepresenting the product, the relationship will fail.

If a great product is damaged during delivery or if delivery is late or cancelled, the relationship will fail.

If the product is sold properly and delivered properly but it doesn't perform properly, the relationship fails.

If a great product is sold correctly, set up correctly and performs flawlessly but the billing and invoicing is done wrong and the charges are not correct, the relationship will fail.

Do you see the pattern here?

Customer focused means that everyone, in every part of the company, must perform their jobs to the best of their ability. No one part of the company is isolated from the other. Everyone must work together to create the best customer experience.

Even people in product design need to take a look at their designs from a customer point of view so they can gain insight into features and benefits that more customer might want to see in the product. Then they can design more popular products that more people will want and more people will purchase.

All of this comes from a vision. That vision starts with the CEO or the owner and is supported and communicated throughout the company until everyone is aware and trained on what to do and how to do it. This is what is required to become a world class customer focused organization.

This is not something that can be done half way and still be successful. It is also something that cannot be accomplished overnight either. It will take time, it will take commitment and it will take constant attention to make everything better.

And yes, it will take money and resources. But the great thing is that once you reach a certain point, it will not cost you money but instead will save you money. Problems cost companies a LOT of money and customer focused companies almost always experience fewer problems. After a while, the company will develop a better reputation which will translate into more sales and greater profits.

But in the beginning, ownership and management must perform in their roles to provide the guidance and resources needed to reach their stated objectives. If that is done the future will be bright. If this support is lacking the future will include much of the same as what had happened in the past.

Funding a Customer Focused Culture

One of the best things about becoming a customer focused organization, company or individual is that eventually you will save money by reducing problems, saving resources and making everything more efficient. But despite this eventual saving of money and resources, it is going to involve some money and resources to get started.

Becoming customer focused requires more than just telling your customers that they need to be more focused on the customer. There is training involved and attitudes to break down and replaced with new attitudes. There are procedures to be studied and changes to be made. All of this requires time, manpower and money.

Very often we hear that a company wants to be customer focused but after making the commitment expects managers and employees to just figure it out by themselves. While a LOT of customer service is common sense, it is important to understand that even common sense has its limitations.

Because of all of this, we need to understand the need for training and instruction at all levels of the company. We need to introduce concepts and information in an organized and uniform manner so that everyone is on the same page as far as what is to happen in any given situation. This requires that EVERYONE be trained not just a handful of people in one or two departments. This is important because one important goal of any customer focused company is a **uniform customer experience.**

A uniform customer experience means that no matter when a customer walks through the door and no matter who is helping or assisting that customer, they will receive the same level and type of treatment as the customer before them received and also the next customer who comes in with the same situation.

A uniform customer experience is important because we cannot pick and choose who will be served correctly and who will receive less service or lower quality assistance.

We need everyone trained so that whether they are trained by Steve, Paul, April or Marge the customer experience will be the same. More of this later.

In order to train people, we need to understand the expenses required in doing so. We have the cost of the training materials including instructors or multi-media materials and we also have the time required to take that training. We should not expect people to take this training on their own time so it usually is done in groups during normal business hours or on an overtime basis.

If the training is done during normal business hours there might be additional manpower required to replace the services of those taking the training. So if there are 5 people taking the training you might need to bring in a few people to handle their job responsibilities while they train. They, in turn, would do the same while others are training.

Depending on the goals of the company and the desired amount of training, the time each employee can be expected to spend on training can be anywhere from a few hours to a week or more of extensive training. Most of the time the actual time frame will be somewhere in between.

Another expense in the beginning phases of the process is the time and manpower spent on evaluating internal policies and procedures in order to decide which are customer friendly and which are not. Depending on the size of the company involved, this can be a very time consuming process. We also need to realize that this is something that should not be rushed because changes should only be made once and not constantly so that employees can keep track of what they are supposed to do in any situation.

Sometimes this particular exercise is done by people outside the company who can come in and look with unbiased eyes so that their judgment is pure and not influenced by corporate culture. The very process of looking at every rule, policy and procedure can involve the challenging of particular corporate attitudes and challenging the views and ideas of fellow employees. Since some people take criticism and change better than others, outside people are often selected to perform this audit in conjunction with internal employees who can explain the need and purpose behind each item.

From the very beginning, through the entire process there will be a learning curve. People will be constantly challenging themselves to follow the new approach or work within the new guidelines. There will be some confusion, some hand holding and a slight decrease in productivity while people learn something new and perhaps struggle to implement it. This is to be expected and there is a cost associated with this learning period. But over time this will become less and less of a factor until it becomes not an issue at all.

I strongly suggest that before a customer focused initiative is announced or started, that every company get a pretty detailed accounting of what it is going to cost in order to train and prepare the company for the new approach. Then add a little to the figure and appropriate the required funds. This is important because you want to be able to do this once and do it right. People usually do not respond well to constant change so the more you can do right the first time the better off everyone will be.

We also realize that some companies might not have the resources to do the kind of job they really want to and that is understandable. In those cases it is perfectly fine to implement the program in stages as funding becomes available.

When done in stages a company can address the area's most urgently in need of attention first and then gradually move on to other areas.

This approach is preferable to not doing anything at all but it also has its pitfalls. Whenever you do anything in stages there will be times when you have to do something over again as situations surrounding it have changed. For example, you might train employees first but not have enough money to evaluate and change policies and procedures. In those cases you will be asking your employees to do business with one set of instructions even though your policies and procedures are not aligned with those instructions quite yet.

Regardless of what approach you take or what time frame might be involved, I urge you to not try and cut corners and do the job right the first time. Be careful and be thorough. Take the time to look at everything and create the best possible rules policies and procedures as possible. Do not focus as much on the costs at this point because doing things right the first time will be cheaper than having to redo things later.

In summary, there will be costs involved in becoming customer focused. You need to be aware of these costs going in but you should also be aware that eventually these costs will lessen and eventually go away.

At that point you should see your business become more productive and not creating nearly as many problems and issues as it once did.

When this happens you begin to reap the savings that come with increased productivity and reduced costs. When that happens you can sit back and smile and congratulate yourself for taking the action you did regardless of the costs incurred in doing so.

Providing Customer Focused Tools

Just like a great carpenter or engineer needs good tools, if you want to become a great customer focused organization you need to give everyone the tools they need to accomplish that goal. You simply cannot just claim to be customer focused, or tell someone to start being customer focused and expect to get acceptable or even marginal results.

With that in mind, we need to figure out what kind of tools our employees might need. After all, every company is different and what might work well for one company might not work for another. The following is a list of some of the tools you might wish to provide to every employee so that they can function at a high customer focused level:

Training

Whenever we ask or expect anyone to some something new or different, we should be supplying those people with the training they need to do their task correctly. After all, you would not want your car repaired by someone who didn't know a steering wheel from a wiper blade and your customers are too important to let guesswork guide your efforts.

Training can take place in many different ways. You send employees out to seminars or bring someone in from the outside to train your employees on site. Seminars usually work well for management before the program is released to the rest of the company because a seminar can expose managers in charge with creating the initiative with added ideas and important points they might not have been aware of.

Employees can also be provided with instruction manuals so that they can learn through reading. This is usually the least expensive option but it still can be very effective. One nice thing about a book or manual is that it is always there for reference or re-reading at any time in the future. But if you go the reading route then there has to be some way of confirming that the employee actually read the manual.

Unfortunately some employees might not share your passion for the new direction and just not take the training or read the manuals.

Training videos are good options as well because they can actually show you how people should look and act when it comes to interacting with customers. You can learn about voice tone and inflection as well as body language and attitude through a video. In our opinion videos work best when used in conjunction with a manuals. In that arrangement people usually read the manual first and follow it up with the appropriate video. This uses more of our sense in the learning process and helps with overall understanding and retention. Videos can also be shown in groups which makes it easy to train several people at once and also make it easier to make sure that employees actually see the video.

Whatever form of training you decide, there needs to be a way to confirm that each employee actually did take the training class or read the manual and watch the videos. You might come up with a short test highlighting some of the material or hold s type of group discussion afterwards. As we already said, there will be some employees who will try and skip the training because they either feel they don't need it or just don't feel it has value.

Training is extremely important because we want every employee to have the same skill sets and knowledge so that every customer receives not just the same level of service but the same type of service. We want every situation handled in the same manner under the same guidelines and with the same intent. Training everyone eliminates the chance of every employee following their own independent approach t customer service.

Reference Materials

Training is very important but after the training is completed most of us will still need additional materials or "cheat sheets" to help us through the period when we try to implement the new knowledge we just received. Anytime anyone tries something new there will be a time frame when we are not sure and our efforts are awkward and less polished. Having something to reference when we need it can be very important.

In most cases it really helps to have a short pamphlet or book outlining how customers are to be treated and what the company expects you to do at every level of the company. This should include information on what the company hopes to accomplish and how it expect to go about accomplishing it.

There should be a clear direction given to everyone for most of the common situations. Employees should have something they can look up whenever they find themselves in a situation where they are not sure what to do next. This book or pamphlet can help a great deal.

This book should be issued to each employee or at the very least one copy per department that is easily accessed by everyone as they need it. One per employee is best because access is much easier and employees are more likely to take the time to read it and use it if access is easy. The more difficult it is to get to it the less it will be used.

This is even more important for people who interact with customers over the telephone. If an employee has the manual or reference guide at their desk, they can take it out and consult it while on the phone making it easier and better to help the customer in the way the company intended. After all, it is always better to do things right the first time.

Clear and Detailed Policies and Procedures

A customer focused company does things pretty much the same way all the time. Granted certain situations might be a little bit different and require a slight modification along the way but the overall approach or starting point should always be the same.

In order to accomplish this, we need to develop and distribute clear and detailed procedures and policies that our employees can used as the framework for how things should get done. These rules and procedures give the employee a path to go down every time they have to deal with a problem or request. This path helps ensure that every customer gets the same level and type of treatment regardless of who handles the request.

When creating these rules and procedures keep in mind that they need to be fair and protect BOTH that business and the customer. They should not be so one-sided that the business always comes first and the customer feels like a distant second or worse. But they should also protect the business so the health and well-being of the business remains protected as well.

These rules and procedures need to be specific and highly detailed. The more specific and detailed we make them the more likely it will be that they are followed properly. Any time we leave it for the employee to interpret what they read or have to figure out what something means, the more likely we are to get different answers and take different actions.

So take the time to create rules and procedures for all the most common situations and actions that employees usually encounter in their jobs. Some of these might include return policies, discount policies, exchange policies, complaint escalation, billing processes, and any other information you feel is relevant to an employee's position in the company.

These rules and policies should be enclosed in an employee handbook of sorts so that they can be easily referred to. There can also be more than one of these manuals or books as well. You might have one book directed at customer service employees while accounting and billing have another book. Or, you can have one master book so that everyone will have access to the information they need whenever a customer needs that information.

Keep in mind that any written publication is subject to legal implications so make sure the rules and policies and procedures you create follow the law and the appropriate customer rights. But if you are honestly and truly becoming customer focused, you probably won't have to worry about that at all. But check anyway!

A Customer Database & Information System

Very often the decisions we make and how we handle certain customers and specific situations will depend on the history of that particular customer.

Having a way for employees to access customer information and history can help them make better and more informed decisions based on that information.

We have already talked about the value of the customer and how that could factor in what we do in order to keep that customer happy. It makes sense that you would want to go further and do more to keep a $1,000,000 customer happy than you might want to do to keep a $5 customer happy. It just makes more sense to the business because there is so much more at stake for the future of the business.

A computer system that can pull up customer data will make it easier for the employee to pull up contact information, details on previous orders and other information that the customer might not have or know how to find. Even more important, it will help the employee be even surer that the information they have is accurate and might even save having the customer sent home to get information that is needed to resolve their problem.

For example, if a customer has an issue with a product and needs a replacement part, if your records have the serial number and date of purchase then you wouldn't have to send the customer home for that information.

You can resolve the information right then and there and the customer will appreciate that you have all of their information on file.

Or maybe there is a warranty issue where the customer needs the date of purchase and he doesn't have it anymore. You can just look it up and give it to them right on the spot. Since we all understand that the faster you can resolve an issue the happier the customer is likely to be, all of this just makes sense.

Having all of this information at your fingertips allows you to improve the level of service you provide to your customers. It also gives you the ability to access even more information that can save your customers important time.

For example, you could have technical or parts information and manuals on your computer so when a customer has a problem, he doesn't have to contact the manufacturer, they can come to you. While this might not be a big deal, it will be one more service you can offer the customer at little or no cost. On the employee side, having this information will allow them to make more accurate statements and decisions which will cause fewer problems and delays down the road.

We live in an information age and our customers expect us to have all of their information on file.

They do not want to have to furnish their personal information every time they come in or call. They expect us to have it and if we want to provide the level of service that our customers expect from us, we need to have a system capable of delivering that information when we need it.

If certain customer information is desired to be kept private or confidential, the system can be password protected with each employee being given access only to the level of information they require in their function. Anything above that level could be accessed upon request by a supervisor or manager as required.

A Customer Friendly Phone or Messaging System

When it comes to becoming customer friendly, an argument could be made that the first contact the customer has on any visit or interaction with our company is the most important. After all, the first part of any conversation or experience sets the tone for most of what follows. Set the right tone and things run smoothly. Set the wrong tone and you will wind up spending more time and resources just trying to get the customer back to where he felt when things got started.

For most companies that do business either online or by phone, and even for companies with brick and mortar stores that do a lot of business over the telephone, the type of phone system they use is critical. This is because nothing aggravates a customer more than an endless chain of prompts and messages that keep them from getting to the person they want or the information they need.

To be a customer friendly telephone answering system, the system must be designed and configured to get the customer where they need to go as quickly as possible. There should be a limited number of options and limited number of questions or prompts. The system should function as an easy and efficient way for customers to be connected with those people who can help them. It should not be designed or used as a roadblock between the company and the customer.

For example, if you have 47 options in your system and your customer needs option 46, he or she is likely to hang up before that option is even identified! Limit your options to as few as 3 or 4 and break things down from there. This will help keep your customer from getting angry or impatient.

Your phone answering system should also have a way for any customer to speak to a real person. This can be by pressing the operator key or by saying "representative" or some other method but there should always be a way to talk to a real person.

If a customer just gets sent to one prompt after another and is finally told to leave a message, I guarantee you that customer is going to walk into your store angry and frustrated.

Another important aspect of a customer focused telephone system is wait time. If your customers have to spend an eternity on hold, they will either hang up or greet the person who finally answers the call with an angry voice and attitude. Wait times short be as short as possible.

A common misconception is that a few minutes of waiting should not be a big deal. But do something for me right now that will better help you to understand. Stop reading and look at your watch or a clock with a second hand. When the second hand hits 12 just stare at the clock or watch and don't do anything else. Don't look anywhere, don't close your eyes and don't think about anything else. Just stare.

See how long a minute can actually seem like? Now multiple that by 5, 10 or 15 times to see what time on hold really feels like to a customer. Wait time is bad for a few reasons. First, it angers the customer. Second, and sometimes most important, the time spent on hold is time spent about the problem they are having.

The more time they think about it the bigger that problem becomes in their mind. So when the agent finally does answer, that little problem is now much larger and will be that much more difficult to resolve.

Having a feature that gives the approx. wait time is a good feature because it helps set a certain expectation in the mind of the customer. It also gives them some constant feedback as to how they are progressing. It also gives them the ability to decide to call back later when the wait times will be less. The more control you give the customer they better off you will be.

Of course, wait times will be dependent on how well the phone system is staffed. Keep an adequate level of manpower so that wait times are always reasonable under normal conditions. Granted there will be times when the system is more heavily used but most customers will understand that. But if they call you 5 times and there are long wait times every time that will get them angry.

Last, but certainly not least, is to provide the ability for every customer to be able to leave a message. This way if the hold times are too long or a certain person or department is out or at lunch, they will not have to start all over. They can just leave a message with a call back number.

Then just make sure that you return those messages in a timely manner. Within an hour is best but no message should go longer than 24 hours. Same day is a good compromise for most businesses. However if the nature of your business is health or safety related, then speed and proper staffing is of the utmost importance. You can delay in responding to someone whose sound system isn't working just right but you cannot wait 24 hours to respond to the person having chest pains!

Company Specific Goals and Objectives

In order for everyone to behave and act the same way we need to have clear guidelines and a clear vision. We already discussed clear and specific rules and policies but understanding the goals and objectives of what the company is focused upon and what their long term goals are can make all the difference when it comes to how employees function.

That is why it is so important to deliver to every employee a clear definition of what the company wants to see in relation to customer treatment and customer satisfaction. The employees WANT to know how to do their jobs. The WANT to know what they should do in any given situation. In other words, most employees WANT to do the right thing!

They just need to know what the right thing is and how they are expected to achieve it!

Don't assume the employees know what is expected of them and what their goals should be. Let them know in a nice way what you think the company is capable of both now and year or 5 years from now. Show them the vision you have for the company and how you plan on achieving that vision.

Most people will embrace change and extra effort as long as they see the reason behind and the ultimate objective. It is not usually enough to ask people to follow blindly just because you ask them to. It is also not enough to order someone to do something without giving them the reasons behind it. When you follow that path, you might get people to comply but they will not give their best effort or get the best results. People usually need a reason to ignite their passion and to give their best.

Give them that reason.

An Escalation Chart or Process

All situations are not created equal and all customers are different so it stands to reason that there will be times or situations where an employee either will not be able to resolve a problem or will not have the authority to do so. When these situations occur, there needs to be a clear and detailed plan in place for the employee to follow.

This plan or process is usually called an **escalation procedure** and it shows employees where to go and what to do when certain situations are encountered. This escalation procedure would outline the situation and then tell the employee who to contact next and what parameters they should use to determine what should happen next.

For example, if a customer comes in with a return request that is outside the return time frame, the escalation procedure would direct the employee as to whether or not to accept the return and what conditions would apply to accepting the return or who to contact for management or other approval. Armed with this information the employee can seamlessly proceed to the next step without having to ask someone else what to do.

The escalation procedure would also give contact information for issues or problems regarding any department or group within the company. So if a customer comes in with a billing problem or inquiry, there will be a contact name and number in the escalation policy for someone in billing. The same would apply for scheduling, delivery, credit, sales, service and any other group or part of the company.

Last, but certainly not least, is an escalation procedure based on the cost of resolving the issue. Naturally if a customer is demanding something that will cost the company a lot of money, the employee is not likely to have the authority to grant that request. So the escalation procedure might outline the contact for the person capable of approving amounts based on that amount. There might be a manager for issues less than a certain dollar amount up to the President or CEO for extremely high dollar amounts.

Though the numbers need not be specific, the situations outlined should be specific enough so the employee is capable of determining who the correct person is to contact for any given situation. For other type of inquiries there should be one or two people to contact for situation specific information and guidance.

The purpose of the escalation procedure is to furnish options for all employees so they will know and understand the limits of their authority and when to escalate a situation and who to escalate it to. The result is faster and more accurate service to each and every customer while still maintaining the health and future of the business.

Limited Decision Making Authority

Nothing slows down the customer service process than employees with little or no decision making authority.

Having to get approval from a manager or other person just adds time, waiting and frustration to the customer service process.

Things work best when employees are able to resolve issues on the spot or over the phone without having to involve others. This speeds up the process and lets the customer get what they need or are asking for with a minimum of waiting or inconvenience. This also helps reduce the anger levels of the customer and the time required to assist that customer.

But it is also understood that you cannot give an employee unlimited decision making authority because the overall exposure to the business could be extremely high. After all, you do not want even the best intentioned employee to give a customer thousands of dollars in products, services or refunds without having some system of checks and balances in place.

A great compromise to this problem is to assign every employee a dollar threshold as far as making decisions is concerned. Then, if something should come along that is under that threshold, the employee simply makes the decision and handles it the way he or she feels is best.

Afterwards, if the decision is thought to be wrong, the manager or supervisor can discuss the situation with the employee and this becomes a learning process for both manager and employee. In the meantime, the customer has been taken care of and has left happy and satisfied. Using this process helps serve the customer faster and better while still protecting the business by limiting the amount of money and resources involved.

Whenever something above the employee threshold is concerned, the employee simply goes to his or her manager or the person indicated on the escalation list to get approval or an alternate proposal to present to the customer.

Using this process helps serve the customer faster and better while still protecting the business by limiting the amount of money and resources involved. It is also less stressful on the employee because they have a clear directive on what they can and can't do. As long as the employee follows the process, both the business and the customer will have been served well.

On-Going Management Support & Direction

As we go through any change within the company, it is critical that everyone continues to receive the support and direction of the management.

That means supporting employees as they work through the change and continuing to provide positive and reinforcing feedback as the process moves forward.

Sometimes there will be glitches and setbacks and this is expected to happen whenever change is taking place. But when these setbacks occur, it is important to stay the course and not abandon things because you are not getting the results you thought you would get.

It also means that management needs to support and adhere to the policies and rules that are now in place. They cannot disregard them at will because it is inconvenient to follow them due to a certain situation. Management must support employees and lead by example.

When employees see management doing the same things and following the same program and embracing these changes they will eventually buy into them and support them as well. But if they see management circumventing or ignoring the same rules that the rest of the company is supposed to follow, they will soon start disregarding them as well.

It is also important to remember that any change is a constant moving process.

Therefore what we acceptable in the beginning might not be acceptable a month or a year later as things evolve. This needs to be constantly communicated to the employees so they understand the reasons behind these constant changes. They need to see this process not as a single change but as an evolution within the company that will bring about higher customer satisfaction through better treatment of customers.

Yearly Update Training

As far as evolution is concerned, evolution never stops. It is always changing and moving as things change around it. As a company, and even as an individual, we too must constantly change along with our customers and our business. This means continuing to introduce new concepts and new ideas as they become available.

Being customer focused is not a one-time initiative or process. It is something that has to be constantly focused on and delivered home to every employee. As old employees leave and new ones come in, each of these new employees needs to be trained and mentored as well. Eventually the culture will become self-sustaining as long as the commitment and attitude remains.

It is strongly suggested that every employee have some form of follow-up training at least once a year.

Whether it is reading a book, attending a seminar or holding a class within the company, every employee must constantly be motivated to deliver quality customer service and not lose focus.

All of these tools, resources and training enable people to do their best under most any situation. It is like giving them a tool belt full of tools to use to make customers happy, resolve problems and great a great reputation for themselves and the company they work for.

Another way of looking at it is that these tools and resources give them w roadmap towards great customer service. They give direction and clarity to decisions and requests. In other words, they help every employee focus on the customer and make customer focused decisions time and time again.

Rules, Policies & Procedures

Up to now we have talked a lot of rule, policies and procedures. We discussed why they must be fair to both the customer and the business without be overly favorable to either side. The customer's interests must be served so they will be happy and return again in the future while the business must be protected so it can generate profits. Profits enable the business to stay in business and still be there when their customers need them in the future.

Policies and rules also serve as guidelines and help create a framework that every employee must work within so they all do the same thing under the same circumstances. Without this framework operating a business would be sheer chaos if everyone did whatever they wanted whenever they wanted to.

So let's all agree the every business, both large and small needs at least a few rules and procedures in order to create order within the business. So the question now should be "How can we create customer friendly rules and procedures that will be agreeable to both the business and the customer?"

The answer to that is to ask yourself five basic questions whenever you are going to create or evaluate a procedure. Those five questions are:

What is the reason or purpose behind this rule or procedure?

Every rule or procedure has a reason behind it. That reason might be to accomplish a certain task or to make sure everything that is being done is being done honestly and equally. These rules and procedures at one point were created because someone did something or needed something and there was nothing in place to address that issue. So a rule or procedure was created and put into action.

Refund time deadlines were implemented because in the past people tried to return stuff months or years after the purchase date. This was a drain on the business and not fair to the business so a time frame in which returns would be accepted was implemented.

The same would hold true for warranty periods and the exclusions that you see in most warranties.

Price matching rules, bill processes, credit qualifications and dispute resolution all came about because in the past each of these caused problems within the business. Once we understand why these rules and procedures exist we can determine whether or not they still need to exist, whether they can or should be changed or modified and how they can m=be made for customer friendly while still achieving their purpose.

Is it fair to the customer?

This is where we look at things from a customer's point of view to try and determine what the customer reaction is likely to be. We do not want to intentionally create something that angers a customer or just serves the purpose of the business. We want to create rules and procedures that accomplish their goals in a customer friendly manner.

For example, if we want to establish a return policy and we look at it strictly from the company point of view we might come up with a 5 days return policy. This way there will be fewer returns and much fewer refunds and exchanges.

But if we look at it from a customer point of view we would easily see that such a short period of time is extremely restrictive and might even be too short for a defect to actually show up during normal use. Such a short time frame would be likely to anger a customer and might be a legitimate reason for them to go elsewhere.

In this particular example we can make the business more customer friendly by extending the return period from 5 days to 14 or even 30 days. Chances are you will find that there will not be all that many refunds or exchanges even though the time frame that you will accept them has been increased greatly. So because of this you can make things much more customer friendly at very little cost.

You will be surprised how most of the time small or subtle changes are all that is needed to turn rule or procedure into a customer friendly one. When you can do this at little or no cost it just becomes a win-win solution for both the company and the customer. But you will only uncover these needs and changes by looking at things through the eyes of the customer.

Does it protect the business?

As we stated, most rules and procedures are designed to protect the business against some form of behavior or legal exposure. As time goes by some of these rules and procedures become unnecessary or need to be modified so that they still provide the same protection for the business.

If the need for this rule or procedure no longer exists, or if the problem itself has gone away or become irrelevant, consider streamlining your business by eliminating this rule all together. Otherwise decide whether or not to change it or leave it as-is.

How can we make it fairer or better for the customer?

If we find we still have a need for a particular rule or procedure, and we have determined that it is fair to both the business and the customer, you might think that your work is done and that things can be left the way they are.

And you would be wrong.

Any time we evaluate anything, even though it appears to be fine just the way it is, there is always the possibility that it can be made even better. Customers are at their happiest when they get more of what they want or need. Anytime you can give the customer more at little or no cost to the business you should take advantage of that opportunity.

That is the difference between being customer focused and just being a good business.

How does the competition handle this?

One important thing to consider when evaluating the way that you do business is how other similar businesses in your neighborhood or industry handle their business. This is important because there will always be a segment of customers that will compare your company against other companies. When this happen it is important that you compare favorably and measure up nicely.

For example, if you have a 15 day return policy and all the other businesses in town have a 30 day policy, you will be seen as being overly restrictive even if your policy is extremely fair. If you offer 48 hour delivery service and your competition all offer same day delivery, you look worse. Any time another company does something better or more customer friendly your company looks worse in comparison.

Because of this it is a great idea to investigate the rules and policies of your competition as you investigate your own.

See how your business compares and then take action to come out better and more customer friendly in ALL aspects of the business. This is where life-long customers are created!

Customers make their buying decisions based on whatever they feel is the most important to them. So don't concentrate on just one or two aspects of your business. Instead, concentrate on the entire business so that whatever your customer might be looking for that they will find it in your company not somewhere else.

Hiring Customer Focused Employees

Now that we know what we have to do in order to develop a customer focused company, let's discuss how we can go about filling that company with the right kind of employees. These are people who believe in customer service and will do their best to cultivate the relationship between the company and its customers.

Let's stop for a minute to think about the employees who interact with your customers on a daily or regular basis. Usually this will not include upper management and sometimes not even the owners of the company. These people are usually at least partially isolated from the day to day customer issues and interaction.

Because of this an argument could easily be made that those employees who interact with the customers on a regular basis are the most important parts of the company. Especially when it comes to the relationships that the customer develops with that company. Have the wrong people in these positions can cause major trouble for any business.

In most cases, changing the focus of a company towards a more customer oriented culture will require the changing of some of the employees. That is because some people just do not have the interpersonal skills or personality that lends them to customer service. This does not mean that they are bad employees or poor workers. But it can signal that these people are not the ones you want to represent your company to the customer.

The type of person you want to be the face of your company are people who will be well accepted by your customers. These people should be able to create relationships with customers so that they return again and again in the future. In other words, your employees should be able to relate to your customers and your customers should be able to relate to your employees. When this takes place both the customers and the company flourish.

With this mind, here are a few things you should look for when selecting the best employees for any position in your company:

Pleasant Personality

Those employees that directly interact with customers in any capacity need to have a pleasant personality. They need to be able to inspire trust and confidence from the very beginning and get the customer to trust them.

Often customers will start an interaction with some suspicion and wariness until they form an opinion about the person they are talking with. If they feel positively towards that person the suspicion recedes and a comfort level is generated.

People with pleasant and friendly personalities tend to draw people in much faster than those who are aloof or distant. We want to bring people in closer so they will open up and share information in a positive manner instead of fighting the process or by being reserved and secretive.

Be Able to Inspire Confidence

Most of the time customer service requires that the customer have confidence in the person who is helping them or trying to resolve their problem or issue. If they do not have confidence in that person they will not believe anything that person might say and they will fight any decision or recommendation that the person brings into the conversation.

In other words, the person has to be able to convince the customer that he or she knows what the heck they are taking about. This means having accurate knowledge of the situation and the products or services involved. It requires the ability to make informed decisions and to make them right the first time so time and resources are not wasted.

In some cases, people are able to inspire confidence even though they might not know what they are doing or how to resolve the problem. But they behave and carry themselves in a confident manner and give the customer the feeling that they will personally do whatever it takes to resolve the problem and make the customer happy.

I worked alongside one employee who was honest and up front with customers. He would tell them that he might not know how to resolve the particular problem but he sure as heck knew a lot of people who could and that he would contact every one of those people until the problem was solved. That is really all the customer really wants. He wants his or her problem solved and if you cannot do it but know someone who does, that's good enough for them.

One of the main aspects of inspiring confidence is appearance. Unfortunately, how someone looks is not always an accurate representation of who that person really is.

But the bottom line is that appearance will affect the level of confidence the customer feels about that individual. This is especially true the first time the customer meets this person.

Though there is a lot to discuss when it comes to appearance of employees for the purpose of this book we will just say that their appearance should be what the average customer should expect from an employee in your type of business. If the employee looks significantly different than what the customer expects that could cause problems.

For example if you were going to invest a million dollars with a financial advisor and he came out in jeans and a dirty t-shirt, would you be impressed? Probably not. But if someone dressed exactly like that came out of the garage to fix your car, you wouldn't think twice. That is because that is what you would expect from an automotive technician but not from a financial advisor.

Another example might be a personal trainer who weighed 400 pounds. How confident would you be that this person was the one who could whip you into shape? How about buying a formal gown from a sales person who was wearing something 3 sizes too small and top that didn't match her pants? Again, you would not be very confident.

This is all about perception. If the customer see what they expect they become more confident. If they see something other than what they expect they will get suspicious and you will have to spend some time to win them over. But some customers will not even give you the chance because they will just walk out and go somewhere else.

Keep in mind that I am not recommending or endorsing hiring anyone by discriminating against any one for any reason. But keep in mind what your customers are going to expect when you choose the employees who are going to interact with your customers. If they do not inspire confidence, do not hire them!

Empathetic & Caring

Over the years I have worked with some of the most talented and skilled people you would ever want to meet. But some of those people were pretty bad at customer service because they were "by the book" people who had or showed little empathy whatsoever towards the customers and their needs or problems.

Customer service is more than knowing what to do in order to make a customer happy. In fact, the biggest part of customer service is how you make the customer feel about YOU, not the product or service.

Customers need to feel engaged with the person trying to help them and they need to feel that the employee is engaged in their problem and aware of how serious it is.

It is amazing how much a situation changes when the employee apologizes for the problem and takes ownership of it. Notice I said ownership and not blame. Those are two entirely different things. You can express regret and sadness over a problem without accepting the guilt. But expressing sadness and taking ownership of the problem can change the viewpoint of the situation immediately.

Think about how an angry customer might feel after getting the runaround by others but then someone from your company tells them "I'm sorry that you are having this problem. Let me see what I can do to resolve it for you." Those words tend to dissolve anger and sometimes even bring upon a feeling of relief that someone is finally going to help them.

Caring and empathetic people often tend to go further in order to satisfy a customer. It is easy enough to say that someone is 3 days out of warranty or that it isn't their job. But it is the special person who goes the extra mile to make sure a customer is satisfied. These are the people you want in your company taking care of your customers!

You cannot force someone to care about other people. This is something that is contained within the personality of that person. In most cases you either have it or you don't. You can't fake it and you can't will yourself to do it either. It is either within you or it isn't.

Helpful and Engaging

I cannot tell you how many times I have walked into a store only to find employees leaning on the counter or talking in the back and ignoring me and the other customers. Or the times I have asked someone for help and received an impassioned "It's over there in aisle 12" type of answer. That is not what you want for your business.

You want people who are go-getters and pro-active. You want the person who doesn't tell the customer where something is located. You want the person to SHOW where it is and answer the questions the customer might have about the product. You want people ready and willing to share their knowledge and expertise with the customers.

Some people just seem to have these characteristics in their DNA. They are committed and impassioned when it comes to the products and services offered by the company. They are eager to get involved and are committed to making certain the customer gets the right product for their needs and to resolving any problems that might occur in the future.

These are the kind of people who will take your customer satisfaction to the next level and beyond.

Committed & Ethical

Perhaps the single most important characteristic of any employee in a customer focused company is honesty and integrity. People need to believe in the products and services and behave in an honest and ethical manner when selling them or servicing them.

This means providing accurate and factual information and not telling the customer something just because it is what they want to hear or to just close a sale. It means having the integrity to stick to what is right even though it might cost you a sale. It means being honest enough to tell a customer that you don't have what he needs but that another business does. Things like this customers remember for a long time.

This is even more important today than at any other time because it seems that there are more and more people out there every day trying to cheat and scam people out of their money. Because of this customers are looking for honest people they can trust and honest businesses they can depend upon.

You cannot run an honest business with dishonest people. You will only get one chance to prove you are honest and reputable. If you lie or cheat a customer once they will likely not give you a second try. At least I know I wouldn't.

Run your business with honesty and integrity. Market your products honestly and treat your customers fairly. Hire people who subscribe to this philosophy. If you find people who are willing to take a shortcut in order to close a sale, be very careful. These are not the people you want as the face of your business.

So now that we know the characteristics of the type of people we want interacting with our customers, how do you go about finding them?

Well, existing employees are a good source of candidates because you already know something about them. After that a personal reference by a current employee is a good source as well. But perhaps one of the best sources of quality employees might be right underneath your nose.

Go out to your competition and other businesses in the area and see how their employees treat you as a customer. If they exhibit most or all of the characteristics we discussed in this chapter, you might want to offer them a job in your company. After all, they have demonstrated the behavior you wanted and they have no idea who you are or that you are looking for qualified people!

Interviews are also a good way of gauging personalities and customer service skills. If a candidate has a lot of entitlement and superiority in their personality you should pass on that person. But if someone appears to be caring and empathetic, you might have a winner.

Keep in mind, though, that during interviews people give the answers that they think the interviewer want to hear. They study common questions and read books about how these types of questions should be answered. So the answers you get might not be how the person really feels. But go with personality first and gauge how you think your customers would relate to this individual

Rewarding Customer Focused Behavior

One key component about becoming and remaining customer focused is to keep every employee committed and engaged in the process. There is no better way to accomplish that goal than to reward employees who embrace the concept and perform at a high level.

Rewards do not necessarily mean cash although that is almost always universally accepted and appreciated. But rewards can also take the form of contests, recognition or other forms of recognition. The type of recognition is not the most important part. The recognition itself is what really matters.

People like and appreciate being commended or recognized for doing a good job or for achieving a certain goal.

This is not only true at work but in life as well. Think about how you felt whenever you were told that you did a good job or did something well. You felt great! Think about how we teach young children. We praise them constantly when they learn any small task. We cheer them when they learn to walk, when they learn to use the potty and even when they strike out in Little League.

We use praise because praise motivates us to continue to try and do better and achieve more. People respond because we all want and sometimes need the approval and recognition of others to show us that we are doing the right things and doing them well. Recognition is a boost to our ego and make us feel good and stay motivated.

Recognition can come in the form of group recognition and individual or personal recognition. In the early stages of the process group recognition gives everyone an idea of how well they are doing. In the case of starting to be more customer focused, we can recognize certain groups or areas of the company for their progress and share results from surveys, letters from customers, etc. This shows people they are moving in the right direction.

Sharing letters from customers is extremely important because these letters let people know that their efforts were noticed and appreciated by the customer and that all that learning and effort was not wasted. They not only get recognition and praise but they see that what they are actually doing is working and is making a difference. One of the toughest things in life is continuing to do something where you don't actually see any results coming from your efforts. Sharing letters and customer comments tells people that what they are doing is working and is worthwhile.

Recognition can come in the form of a mention in the company newsletter or e-mail. This is an effective way of sharing letters and comments from customers as well. It is effective because employees can save the e-mail or newsletter and even print it out and hang it in their workplace as a gentle reminder that what they are doing works. Not only that, but other people entering that workplace will see it and read it and see the benefits of making the same efforts.

Another form of recognition that is important is recognizing an employee's role in something that benefitted the company. For example, if someone went above and beyond for a customer and that resulted in landing a large order or a new account, then mention that person and what they did in a memo or in the newsletter.

This lets people know that a small effort (or a larger one) can result in big benefits to the company. It is one thing to do something because it was the right thing to do and another thing to see it pay major benefits down the road. Very often we are not aware that the things we do can create such powerful benefits and income for the company. We should let our employees know how what they do influences customer behavior.

If we have a way of measuring the success of our efforts, such as reports or surveys or other feedback that lets us know how our customers feel about our company, we can use that to create contests and award programs where employees have the opportunity to receive a prize or other award for outstanding achievement. This method of recognition is always appreciated and well received.

You could have a contest where the best department or team wins a catered in pizza party or similar reward. Individuals can get prizes or cash awards for being the best or most customer focused. No matter how we reward people, it is the recognition that is the most important. But whenever you place a prize or award in front of people, they usually will focus more and try a bit harder.

Even though the award itself is not important, it should be large enough to motivate people. It should not be so small that the employees view it as cheap or even insulting. The value should be appropriate for the company and the criteria behind the award.

For example, if you have a company-wide customer satisfaction contest that has one winner at the end of the year and that person wins a $10 gift certificate to a local fast food restaurant that is going to be viewed as cheap and insulting by the employees. If there is one winner per year the award should be much more substantial. Since the award signifies the importance that management places on the behavior itself, in that case the size of the award is important.

But if the company does improve and management decides to give everyone that same $10 gift certificate, that might be well received because even though the amount of the gift was small, it did show recognition and appreciation for their efforts. So be aware of the reward offered and the context with which it was given and you should be fine. You don't have to be extravagant but you shouldn't be cheap either!

Last, but certainly not least, don't overlook the power behind a kind word and support from management. If someone did a good job, tell them.

If someone went above and beyond for a customer, let them know their efforts are appreciated and have not gone unnoticed. A kind word from your boss lets an employee know they are doing the right thing or at least heading in the right direction. That is all that a lot of people need to keep doing what they are doing.

Even if someone hasn't gone above and beyond but is still doing the right thing or at least trying, a word of encouragement, and even a little mentoring will help them do even better. Some employees need a little boost once in a while. They need to know they are appreciated. This is what recognition is all about.

If you currently recognize your employees in this manner that is great, just add customer satisfaction and customer care to your recognition program. But if you are one of those managers or owners who feel that keeping your job should be motivation enough, rethink that approach. You want your employees to look at their job as more than just a job and you want them to see your customers as more than just customers. Sometimes recognizing people for their efforts allows them think   properly.

The Role of Management in Customer Service

Now that we have our mission laid out in front of us and we know what we want to do, it is time to put the program together and deliver it to the employees in an easy to understand and easy to implement manner. In some respects, this phase of becoming customer focused is the most critical part and needs to be handled carefully.

Unless you have hired an outside company to create and deliver your customer service training, you are going to need to create the program and deliver the training in such a way that most, if not all, of the employees will be able to take the training and understand it with a minimum of inconvenience.

After all, the easier we make something, the more likely people are going to become involved in it and embrace it. If it is too difficult or cumbersome, many employees are likely to resist it.

Management's role is to create the right program in the right way and roll it out to the company in an organized and controlled manner. After that is complete management's role turn into a support role where they support the program and lead by example. This is not one of those "introduce the program and move on" situations. Management must be engaged throughout the entire process.

Management must also fund the initiative as well and we have discussed this already. No one can expect to implement a new culture and develop new attitudes and new rules without incurring some kind of expense. You can take steps to minimize those expenses to a certain extent but you cannot eliminate them. If you approach the program with that intent, you will fail. It is as simple as that.

In companies where there is multi-level management, the commitment and direction of the program must be present in all levels of management. You cannot have one level of management committed to customer service and another level that places customer service way down their list of priorities. In other words, management must appear, and actually be, united in their vision and support of the program.

Multi-level management also should have every level of management involved in the creation and design of the program as well. Every level of management has a unique perspective on what is required and needed in order to design the best program and have the greatest chance of success in implementing it. Those at the higher levels of management have the benefit of seeing the larger vision and the future of the program. Lower levels of management are more in tune with how employees feel and the actual day to day activities which will have a significant impact on how the program will be carried out by the staff.

In fact, when it comes to what is actually needed, and what problems are actually being faced on a daily basis, the lower level managers are sometimes the most valuable. Because they are closest to what is actually happening between the customers and the company, they are usually the most aware of what needs to be done to create better customer relationships.

So all levels of management should be consulted and involved in developing the program and implementing it.

All levels of management should also be involved in taking the finished program and de-bugging it or working out all the problems or glitches before it is released to the rest of the company. Management needs to be critical of their work and open to criticism from all levels of managers. Lower level managers should be encouraged to point out problems or issues that they see and should not be afraid to speak up. The end goal is not to make upper level management feel good about their work. The end goal should be having the very best program possible by the time it is rolled out to the rest of the company. When all is said and done, all levels need to support the program as it is introduced.

This is important because there will always be a group of employees that will buy into what management says but will still look to see if management is committed to following the same philosophy that the employees are expected to follow. If they are, then things go much more smoothly. But when management tells employees to do one thing while they do another, performance and success are usually negatively impacted.

Management must also function as an evaluator of the program as well. Even the most thought out and well-designed programs need adjustment or tweaking as they are rolled out. Things often do not go as planned so changes in mid-stream are not uncommon. In fact, they are to be expected. So it is not a case of if problems will pop up but instead when they are going to pop up. Then it becomes a matter of how we deal with those problems.

Management must also exhibit patience as changing an entire attitude throughout the company is going to take time. There will be glitches along the way and there will be set backs and problems as well. This is to be expected. There is a learning curve that accompanies the implementation of anything new and this is to be expected.

People learn at different rates and there will be different levels of compliance and success throughout the company. Some employees will "get it" or buy into the change sooner than others. This doesn't mean the people who take longer are poor employees or not putting in the required effort. Instead, it just means that some people are slower to respond to change than others. So we will need to have patience and look at the long term prognosis instead of the short-term performance.

Management also needs to function as a coach throughout the process as well. That means bringing the changes to the employees in a very positive manner that is designed to make it easy for employees to learn about what is happening and how they can be a part of it. We have said it several times already but just telling someone to do something is not enough. You must show them why the changes are necessary and also give them the tools they need to create the skills sets required.

A coach will act as a role model and exhibit the type of behavior that they want to see from the rest of their team. That means the managers at all levels should practice the techniques they want to see their employees use. This way the employees can observe what their managers are doing and model that behavior. The manager also acts as a source of feedback to let the employees know when they are doing things right and also when things need to be done a bit differently.

Last, but most certainly not least, management must take their program and allow it to operate in a real-world environment. Business is not perfect and sometimes goals do not align with each other. When this occurs management must not insist that employees meet goals that are counter-productive. This can only lead to confusion and frustration.

For example, if you need more manpower to reduce customer wait time and handle more customers in less time, then you should not expect a manager to hire people while holding the salary budget at the current levels. You either place the priority on adding manpower for higher customer satisfaction. You cannot add manpower while keeping costs stable.

A perfect example would be something I frequently ran into when I managed a group of dealers who serviced our products. The management of the dealers told their technicians that they wanted them to spend more time doing service so they could get more jobs done every day. But then they added other, non service related, responsibilities to the same technicians that resulted in giving them less time each week to dedicate to service! In that case management told them to do more and then gave them less time to do it with! Needless to say, they failed miserably.

We mentioned real-world and it would be remiss to not state that there is nothing more real-world than customer behavior and customer satisfaction. Customer behavior cannot be totally described on paper and there is no one size fits all solution or approach to customer service. Instead, every customer is different and every company is different.

So all we can do is arm ourselves with the most information we can possibly get and learn as much about our business and our customers as possible. Then we make the most informed decisions possible and implement them to the best of our ability. But then we monitor everything and we become patient. We see what works and embrace that and let it continue to work. We see what doesn't work and we try and figure out what went wrong. Then we make some changes and try again. Over time, and with patience, we will be rewarded with the results that we wanted from the beginning.

But only if management is patient and only if management sets the right example and models the right behavior. At the risk of further repeating ourselves, customer service is not something that can be commanding or ordered. It has to be taught and it has to be created.

How an Individual Can Create A Customer Focused Environment

So far we have concentrated on how a company can implement a customer focused environment and structure within the entire company. But individuals can also have a significant impact within a company or in their own careers when it comes to customer service.

As we have said many times so far, customer service is more of an attitude than a skill. In fact, it is an attitude that uses several skill sets to satisfy a customer and make him more likely to return and recommend the individual or business to their friends and other people. Because it is an attitude, it is something that can be done on an individual level even if not embraced or practiced by the rest of a company.

Customer service skills, or soft skills as they are sometimes referred to, are among the most valued and sought after skills by Human Resource people and Recruitment professionals. That is because people who possess these skills are usually more productive and perform at a higher level than those who do not have these skills. So it is safe to say that those people who possess the skills required to provide a higher level of service will be in higher demand than those who don't. So if you are looking for motivation or a reason to go out and develop these skills, you have just found it!

Because customer service is an attitude more than anything else, individuals, whether part of a company wide effort or just something they wish to do for themselves, need to change the way they look at their job and the way that they do it. They must change their focus from being a bottom line, follow the letter or the law type employee to one who takes the customer's needs into consideration more.

We should stop right here to say that if this is something you are doing on your own and not as part of a company mandated or sponsored initiative, you must still follow the rules, policies and procedures of the company while you are doing your job.

You can still look at things from the customer' point of view when making your decisions but those decisions still must fall within the established guidelines of doing your job. You can suggest changes with your superiors but it is not your place to willingly go against policy on your own because you feel it will help the customer.

But training yourself to consider the impact on the customer before making your decisions is one of the most effective ways of becoming more customer focused. Individuals usually have more than one option when it comes to handling situations and it just makes sense to look at all sides before making your decision. While some might just think of the business and the impact on the business when making their decisions, you can also factor in the impact on the customer into your decisions as well.

Often times this will guide you to making a choice that is more favorable in the eyes of the customer while still protecting the needs of the company. In other words, you will find yourself helping both the business and the customer at the same time. This is called a "win-win" resolution and it should be the goal of every resolution. When both the customer and the business are happy with the resolution, you have done your job wonderfully. When only one party is happy, you might have been able to do better. While nothing is ever 100%, you need to always search for the win-win resolution.

As far as individual efforts are concerned, the one thing you need to always remember is that you can only control what you do. You cannot expect others to join your efforts or support what you are doing. This is something that you have decided to do on your own so you are on your own.

But that doesn't mean that you cannot take the initiative and develop better and stronger relationships with the customers. You can do your best to help them with their problems and address their needs to the best of your ability. As long as you adhere to company policies and procedures you should be just fine.

One way that individuals can change the culture of the company on their own is by taking certain behaviors that have proven to work and be effective and showing others how doing those things have made things easier, better or more productive. When it comes to most people, if you show them how they will personally benefit by doing something different they will usually at least give it a try.

That is one of the keys in getting people to do something new or different. Basically you are selling them on an idea. Part of the basics of selling involve selling people on the benefits of buying or doing something.

Once you show a person how something new or different will make their life or job easier or better, they will usually be receptive.

The better results you can produce the more appealing it will be to others and the more people that will take notice. When enough people see the benefits to what you are doing, it will not take long for it to become noticed by management. That is where your personal efforts can affect change in the entire company.

When it comes to individual efforts another difference is that getting the training you need to learn how to be more customer focused might not be paid for by the company. I would approach your boss or the person who approves certain expenses and ask them anyway but be prepared for a rejection. This is because some people honestly believe that such training and the skills you will learn will not benefit the company financially. While this is 100% wrong and totally off base, it is still something a lot of managers believe.

That means as an individual that you will have to pay the costs of the training. But that should not be a deterrent because you can learn a lot with a very modest investment. You can get a complete set of Customer Service manuals from the Customer Service Training Institute (www.infowhse.com) for less than $40 (shameless plug but still a great deal!) and this will give you everything you need to get started.

These skills are important and will definitely make you more productive and more valuable to the company at the same time. These skills also translate well into other parts of your life as well. Remember, customer service is all about communication and communication is important for all kinds of relationships.

This is one area where one person can make a big difference. Success is contagious and other will climb on board once they see the results you produce. So get the knowledge, implement it in your job, watch the results and see others join you. When that happens you will know that you did your part to help create a customer focused attitude and culture in your department.

The rest of the company comes next!

The Whole Company Needs to Be Focused on Customer Service

Let's get into a bit more detail about something we have discussed a bit so far and that is why it is so important for the entire company to be customer focused and not just the people who come in daily or direct contact with the customer. This is important because this is one of the most common, yet potentially most deadly, mistakes that companies of all sizes make when it comes to customer service.

On the surface, it might make sense, when it comes to customer service, to train just the people who sell or service the customer. After all, these are the people who talk to the customers and handle their requests, problems and other things for them. But the problem with that logic and approach is that the people who interact with the customers do not act in a vacuum or handle everything themselves.

Eventually parts of the process or resolution will be handled by other people who, under this approach, will not receive the training and might not be customer focused. When this happens, the same thought process and care that was exhibited by one employee might not carry through to the next and so on. A weak link in the customer service process develops and when even a single link breaks, the entire process falls apart.

For example, let's say a customer calls with a billing problem. A payment they made was not credited to their account on the date when it should have been. The result was late charges that the customer wants removed from his account. As a customer focused employee you express empathy and concern and forward the problem to a person in the billing department because they have access to individual account records and you do not.

Now Mary over in the billing department is not customer focused and was never a part of the customer focus initiative because she sits at her desk behind the scenes and rarely interacts with customers. So the company figures it was not a smart use of resources to furnish her with skills she would rarely use.

So the request comes in and Mary looks at it and decides that she has far too many more important things to do so it goes on the bottom of the pile. After all, Mary doesn't realize that customer problems get worse as time goes by. All she knows is that as long as the charges are removed by the end of the current billing cycle, everything will be fine. So she handles the more important things first and lets this customers quote sit there for over a week.

Mary doesn't look at this issue from the customer's point of view and doesn't realize that the customer is concerned, possibly worried, that their payment was not credited to their account. All they see are the late fees that were charged and that no payment was credited. Because of this Mary doesn't call them to let them know everything will be fine and that they will receive an updated statement next period.

But at home the customer goes on their online account page every day, sometimes two or three times a day, to check their account to see if the correction has been made. Every day they don't see the correction they worry more. Every day they don't receive a call they get more upset. Finally, after about a week without seeing the update or receiving a call, they call back. But now they are angry that nothing was done.

So a minor or innocent issue has now turned into a major issue and the customer who once was calm and patient is now angry and upset.

Not because Mary is a bad employee or because Mary did something wrong but because Mary was not aware or trained to look at things from the customers point of view. So she missed doing something minor that could have made the entire issue go away.

Had she looked at the issue from the customer's point of view she would have realized that a simple phone call to the customer would have made everything all right if that call had been made the same day or the next day after the customer reported the problem. But she didn't consider the customer's feelings or problems so that call was never made. So the homeowner thinks no one is helping them.

People who are trained in customer service understand the need for doing things quickly and keeping customers informed every step of the way. They understand that the longer a problem is allowed to exist, the larger it becomes in the minds of the customer. So it is very easy for a little tiny issue to become a major problem if it is allowed to go on for too long.

In this example there will be no impact to the customer as long as Mary makes the correction within the next 3 weeks.

But because the customer doesn't know this, they conjure up all of the extra fees and effort it is going to take to resolve a problem that really isn't there. So even though there isn't a problem, the customer perceives there is one and that perception becomes their reality.

Now some of you reading this book are thinking that because the perception isn't real or accurate it is not their problem. After all, why should we have to be held accountable for something that is just existing in the mind of the customer? Why should we have to deal with something that doesn't exist? People who were trained in customer service and that are customer focused would not ask those questions because they know the answer.

We are not going to go into all the reasons for having everyone trained because that would take too long and would be too boring to those not particularly interested in that. But there is one answer that will take all of those reasons and combine them into one big reason why everyone should be customer focused within the company.

That one reason is:

We should never give any customer any reason to even think about going elsewhere or even make them consider checking out the competition.

This is important because whenever we give our customer any reason, no matter how small, to look elsewhere we dramatically increase the chances that we will lose that customer in the future. That is the last thing we ever want to do.

Every time a customer thinks they might get a better deal or better service somewhere else, their natural inclination is to go and check out someplace else. When they walk into that store the employees and management of that store are going to bend over backwards to welcome a new customer and gain their business. Your customer will see only the good things and not the bad.

Your customer will also have a somewhat negative feeling about you and your business right now anyway and that alone might result in your customer "giving them a try" to see how things go. Since many of us are creatures of habit, that "try" might easily turn into a lifelong relationship.

A long time ago I had a friend who fixed electronic equipment for a small chain of stores. It was a great job for him and he made a ton of money and he only had to work a few hours a week to make that money. But one store owner always paid late and avoided him when he owed him money.

But eventually he always paid him. But it was annoying and my friend sent him a letter stating that if invoices were not paid on time in the future they would be sent to a collection agency.

The store owner got mad and looked for another company to do their service. He found on and that person was very good. Eventually store by store the entire chain switched to the new company and my friend lost a lot of income that he never got back. All because he gave someone a reason to look elsewhere for their service.

Imagine if someone in your delivery department made a mistake because they weren't trained and didn't know better. Maybe they said the wrong thing or had a customer unfriendly rule or process still in place. Or, maybe the people who designed the products didn't bother to read customer comments or complaints and kept on creating products that customers didn't like?

It makes no difference where an error or problem originates in the customer experience. If a problem pops up midway through by someone who doesn't understand the importance of something, the entire experience can go bad very quickly.

But despite this, many companies fail to realize the importance of training everyone in the company in customer service. All they see are the savings in resources and their minds become made up and nothing will change them.

But there are alternative or options available that can help get everyone trained while saving resources. Here are a couple of things you might want to consider if you cannot afford, or just don't want to pay for everyone to be trained:

Tiered Training

With tiered training, not everyone receives the same level of training. The employees who deal directly with customers every day would receive the most comprehensive and detailed training while those employees who rarely interact with customer would receive a basic overview. The overview would be enough to make them aware of the concepts and fundamental so they would know how to develop customer awareness

IN this approach, the cost to train all of the employees who do not have customer interaction on a regular basis would be much less. It would also take less time. For example to train a customer service representative might take a week of classes while the overview might be able to be done in a single day or maybe even a half day. It is not ideal but it will give every employee exposure to the need to think of the customer when making any decision.

Staggered Training

In this approach everyone receives the same training but at different times. The employees with the most customer contact would go first and then other employees would go later. While this might not save any money, it will spread out the cost of training over a longer period of time so the charges will not hit the budgets all at once.

The benefit of this approach is that everyone gets the same training so everyone should be pretty much on the same page when it comes to knowing what to do and how to do it. This helps provide a more uniform level of service without confusion or misunderstandings.

The negative about this approach is that it takes longer to train everyone and until everyone receives the training the chances of mistakes happening and problems being created will be greater. But even with that considered, training everyone, even though it will take longer, is still more important.

Leader Training

This approach is not the best but it is better than no training at all. In this approach every department sends one or two people to the training and then it is their responsibility to bring what they learned back to everyone else. This way everyone gets exposed to the materials but the cost is much lower.

There are a few pitfalls to this approach that you need to be aware of.

First and foremost, when you expect someone to train others you must send the right person to the training. Not everyone can train other people and if you send someone who is not capable of teaching others then there will be gaps in the training.

Second, when you have people training others they often will not present the same material in the same manner. Some material might get left out or presented in a different way that is more difficult to understand. When this happens not everyone will get the same training and misunderstandings can arise.

Third, different people will interpret the same information or statements differently. When every person attends training this is no big deal because just that one person's viewpoint is affected. But when we send one person to the training and then expect them to train a group of others, they will teach the other according to what they interpreted the instructor said.

We also run the risk of the one person injecting his or her feelings or even bias into the re-training process as well. Because of this it is important to pick the right person for this task.

While it usually is a manager or supervisor, if there is an employee much better suited to this task then that employee should be sent to the training to make sure everyone gets the best training possible.

As you can easily see, it is important that everyone get some degree of training. This includes management as well because management is going to have to be the ones who support and model the desired behaviors.

No one is too important to take the training.

No one is above taking the training.

No one isn't important enough to take the training.

No position should be exempt from training.

Follow those statements and get everyone trained. This will help ensure that every one of your customers gets the treatment they receive. This will also stop you from giving any customer a reason to look elsewhere.

And that is exactly why all of this training is needed.

Make it Easy to Do Business With Your Company

Today we live in a fast paced world where many things at least appear more complicated and more difficult than they really need to be. One of the objectives when it comes to becoming customer focused is to make your business easier and faster to do business with. This is important because there will always be a segment of your customer base that is looking to get in, get what they need and get out as quickly as possible. If you want to keep these customers as your customers, then you have to make your business more customer friendly.

With this in mind here are a few things most customer feel are important when it comes to doing business with any company:

Ease of Overall Shopping Convenience

There is a store near where I live that has great products at great prices. They also have a selection that is second to none as well. The problem is that I absolutely hate to shop there because it is so difficult to find what you need and get out.

As far as marketing is concerned their store layout borders on genius because there is one entrance and one exist and you have to walk through winding aisle and corridors to get out of the place. So even if you know what you want and know where it is located, you have to walk through the entire store to get there. Then you have to walk through the rest of the store to check out and get out!

While this makes you notice and see every damned product, it also takes a ton of time to navigate through the purchase process. If I had a ton of time it might be interesting to see all that they have but if you are pressed for time or on your lunch hour, you just do not shop there. So the result is that I often pay slightly higher prices elsewhere because those places are easier to deal with.

Store Layout

Probably one of the most important factors when it comes to making it easy to do business with your company is to create a store layout where products are located in a logical and intuitive manner. That means having accessories near the main products and having similar products grouped together and easily identified.

It also means having the most common products in the most prominent locations. While some business design their stores to have the popular products in the rear so you have to walk by their other product to get to them, a customer friendly store will have the most common products on end caps or in other highly travelled or prominent locations. This makes it easier for the customer to come in, find what they need and get on to their next task for the day.

Ease of Access

Even such things as having adequate parking or a location that is easy to get to in every direction helps make your business more desirable for your customers.

Though that doesn't mean that you should pack up and move your business to a better location but it might mean that if you were going to do so that this might be one of the considered factors in determining the best new location for your business.

Keep in mind that the further away your customers are the easier it has to be for them to get to you. Lower prices will not bring someone in from an hour away unless they are going to save a ton of money.

Wait Time

It doesn't matter if customers have to wait for sales help, to pay for their product or just wait on hold for the next available agent, just about every customer just HATES to be placed on hold. Waiting for anything means wasted time and having to take longer to get through all the tasks that lie ahead for the day.

For busy people with cramped or packed schedules, knowing they are going to have to wait is enough to have them look for other places to shop. I know that I will go out of my way to avoid places where I know I will probably have to wait for anything. For me personally, my time is valuable and I will go where I can spend the least amount of time to get what I need.

This meets adequate staffing levels to make sure lines aren't long and that people can get the help or assistance they need when they need it. Sometimes this might mean special scheduling for the busiest times of the day or reassigning workers to different positions to handle peak shopping periods.

Over the phone wait times are especially frustrating because over the phone you cannot see what is going on around you. In person you can see the people ahead of you and can often do other things while you wait. On the phone, however, you are held captive because you never know when you are going to be next. Either way, having enough representatives on hand to keep wait time to a minimum is always a good idea.

Product Selection

Customers like to be able to find what they want, or at least have a reasonable degree of certainty of doing so when they come into your store or enter your website. If they routinely find that your selection is too limited or restricted they will eventually stop coming to you first and will look elsewhere. If they find another place that has what they want when they want it, you probably will lose a customer for good.

This means that you have to know your customers and have what the majority of them will want when they come to you. This means asking questions and being responsive to their answers. If someone comes in and asks if you carry something, then consider adding it to your product line.

Have someone place themselves in the shoes of the customer and ask themselves what products they would like to see carried in your store. Then consider adding some of them to your selection. Customers also like to see different levels and quality of products as well. So if someone needs a widget, you should have an economy widget, a general purpose widget and a deluxe widget. This way the customer gets what they want and you have the best chances of closing a sale.

If you want to go the extra mile for your customers, develop the reputation of getting your customers what they need even if you don't carry it. With computer systems the way they are today just about every product that is still sold today should be within your grasp. If the need isn't urgent so can order the product for the customer, close the sale and keep that customer away from any other business. That is truly a win-win resolution. Except, that is, for your competition!

Become Known as the One-Stop Resource!

I cannot tell you how many times I have gone to a particular company just because I knew that I would get my questions answered, get the products I needed or get a problem resolved no matter what that problem might be. Many of those times I purchased products or services that were priced higher just because of the overall service and faith that I had in the company. This is something that is often overlooked by some companies even though it should be common sense.

A customer focused company understands that just providing information to a potential customer might not immediately result in closing a sale but it will establish a bond between the company and that customer. Whenever you help people they will remember it and appreciate it. They will tell others about their experience and your reputation will spread throughout the community.

Granted there will always be those people who will come in and get the free information and then go buy the product somewhere else because it is 12 cents cheaper. But those people will still tell other people and those people WILL buy products and services from you.

Like most other parts of customer service, the things you do today will help you land more customers and do more business in the future.

If you choose to take this approach it usually means you will have to have a knowledgeable and experienced sales and support staff who will know what they are talking about when a customer asks them a question. But equally important is that they have the contacts and resources to point the customers in the right direction when they do not have the answers. Your goal should be to either solve the customer's problem or at least put them one step closer to getting it solved when they leave. If you ca accomplish that, your customer will soon come to trust and love your business!

The Uniform
Customer Experience

Before we get started on telling you how to start becoming customer focused, we need to once again discuss the need for everyone being trained so that we can provide a constant and uniform level of service no matter who the customer interacts with and regardless of the problems or needs the customer might have. Failing to provide the correct level of service EVERY time is going to lead to unhappy and frustrated customers.

A uniform level of service and experience is the backbone of just about every business. This is especially true when it comes to businesses with more than one location. Franchises do quite well because customers know that whether they walk into a fast food restaurant in California or Maine they are going to get the same food served in the same manner. This builds in a certain degree of confidence and familiarity in the mind of the customer.

After all, why try someplace you know nothing about when you know what you will get in the franchised location?

But even in non-franchised businesses always providing the same level of service to each customer is very important. All we need is one bad experience and we can wipe out the good will and confidence that we had built up over the last several visits. Since the last thing we want to do is give a customer a reason to look elsewhere, we need to keep every customer interaction at a very high level.

The other reason for having a uniform level or service is so every employee handles situations in the same manner. If this does not happen then customers will always try and go to a certain employee who tends to give them more than the other employees. Word gets around and then this one employee becomes suddenly more popular among the customers.

There is also the risk that customers will talk amongst themselves and this happens far more often than one might think. If a customer finds out that someone else with a very similar problem received a much more favorable resolution, then that customer is going to become very upset. Our goal is to have every customer treated in a very similar manner so that if and when they do talk, their experiences will be mostly the same.

Generally speaking the more offices a company has and the more departments the company has in place, the greater need for training to insure that everyone is on the same page as far as what needs to happen in certain situations. People who work side by side can lean on each other for guidance and assistance. But those in other offices or other buildings do not have that luxury. In those situations, the common saying that "the left hand doesn't know what the right hand is doing" often holds true.

The goal of the company should be to arrive at a minimum level of service and customer treatment that EVERY customer will ALWAYS receive when interacting with any employee. This is something that every employee must be committed to and be expected to deliver every time they deal with any customer. In some cases you will supply a higher level of service but under no circumstance would you supply less to any customer. The idea is to provide as uniform and level customer experience possible for all customers.

There are two ways that a business can provide a uniform customer experience. The first is by informing and training every employee about how to interact with customers and how to treat them in various situations.

If everyone is given the same instruction then as long as everyone follows the instructions everyone should be on the same page as far as customer service is concerned. This is where we want to be when training is concluded.

After training the next most important aspect of a uniform customer experience are the rules and procedures that outline specific actions that employees are to follow when dealing with customers. These rules and procedures need to be specific and detailed so there is little leeway for interpretation and guesswork. Even though giving employees room to use common sense and think independently is important when it comes to customer service, there needs to be a solid framework within which all employees must function.

Once these rules and procedures are created and implemented it is up to the managers to make sure they are adhered to by everyone so that every customer receives the same level of treatment and is offered the same, or at least very similar resolutions. This level of enforcement is extremely important and the managers must keep on top of compliance so that everyone continues to follow these rules and procedures.

This does not mean that some customers and some situations might require action outside of these parameters.

But those situations should be the exception rather than the rule. There will always be times when it make sense to go above and beyond but we should always have good and solid reasons for doing so. In the cases of exceptions the managers should be involved in approving any action that goes above and beyond policy.

It should also be understood that a perfect uniform level of service is usually not possible because there will always be people who function at higher levels and other people constantly trying to do the right thing with the best intentions. Whenever this happens the level of service changes. But if you reach a point where you are not sure whether or not you should do something to satisfy a customer it is almost always better to make the call on the customer's side as long as it doesn't exceed policy by too much.

But just try to create a framework that does its best to provide a uniform level of service through departments and throughout the company. This will help reduce problems and make more customers happier with you and your company.

How to Get Started

So now hopefully we understand what needs to happen, why it needs to happen and what our goals or objective are for the process. If we are not at any of those points right now, it might be best to go back and re-read some sections of this book. This is important because you cannot get from start to finish without understand all of those points.

But let's assume you are ready to get started. So the question at this point should be "How do I get started and where do I begin?"

The best way to start any process, or facilitate any change, is to first understand what you are trying to accomplish. You can determine this by asking yourself and your employees a few easy questions. At this point we are in the information gathering stages.

What problems are you trying to resolve?

What negative situations are impacting your business?

What might be coming up in the future that you have to change or prepare for?

What complaints are you or your employees hearing from your customer?

We also would like to have any data or other information that is available to get a feeling of where we currently stand as far as customer service is concerned. Here are a few ways we can access information:

If you currently track customer satisfaction, get the latest reports as well as reports for the last few years so we can spot any trends.

Create an employee survey and distribute it so that we can get input from those employees who directly interact with the customers.

Do an informal exit poll of customers as they leave your store or end a telephone conversation.

Hire a company to do some surveying of your customers and a comparison of your business against similar businesses in your area.

After you have as much information as possible, gather it all together and analyze it.

Spend as much time as you possibly can on this step because the results you arrive at will determine the overall quality of the program and the effectiveness of the results it gets.

After you have all the information and have analyzed it, there are two basic ways that you can proceed. If you have substantial issues or problems with one or two parts of the company, or if you have a significant issue that effects the entire company, then you might want to develop a program and action plan to address those issues first.

For example, if you are getting a ton of complaints about your product quality, then you might want to address those concerns right now rather than wait to make them a part of your overall customer satisfaction program. That is because these problems are specifically causing your business problems NOW and they need to be addressed NOW rather than later. Since the longer problems are allowed to continue or remain, the greater impact they will have on the company. This means more lost customers, greater loss of revenue and more problems for everyone in the company.

If this is the case, design an action plan to address these urgent issues now and implement those changes and procedures to stop the problems from continuing In the future. Once that is done you can start damage control measures to try and restore the effected customer relationships.

If there are no critical or urgent problems then we can take all the data and information and begin to create a comprehensive program designed to change the attitudes of the employees to a more customer focused culture. That means going through policies and procedures and make them more customer focused.

Start with an outline of what needs to be done throughout the company and then break it down to the department level so we know what needs to happen at all levels of the company. Be as detailed and as comprehensive as possible. We can always remove or cut out things later if we feel they are not needed. But the more we have entered the more accurate the "bigger picture" will be.

Another reason for being as accurate and complete as possible is that it is easier to see duplicate problems or issues across department when there are more entries listed. If we see the same issue reported over multiple departments or sections of the company then that would indicate a more serious issue and one that would have greater impact when addressed.

If you have levels of management within the company then roll out the initial draft to each manager and have them work through it and create a program or action items list for their department.

When all managers have completed this all action plans should be evaluated and then rolled back up into one program.

When you have they first draft of the program then have a management meeting where the entire program is examined and "tightened up" as far as removing duplicate or not needed items. You might have to do this exercise a couple of times as the program take on a more defined and accurate format.

Now that we have a defined and accurate program in front of us, the next phase is trying to determine the best way of getting that program implemented throughout the company. Usually there are three primary options as far as how a program will be implemented in the company.

Outsource the Training

The first option is to hire an outside company to take the program and develop a training series to bring to the employees. They will then schedule sessions or webinars to deliver the training to each group. This is the easiest option but it also has a few negatives or pitfalls associated with it.

First and foremost, having another company handle the training for you is expensive.

Quality trainers are not cheap and the number of hours can be considerable depending on the size of the company. But in some cases they might have an "off the shelf" program that they can provide saving you all the development time. If you do not have specific problems or issues and your needs are generic this might work. But if you want a customer program specific to your company, industry and particular needs, it is likely to be expensive.

The other downside is that when someone from outside the company does the training there is a disconnect between the trainer and the people getting trained. The trainer is not intimately aware with your company and how things work on a day to day basis. There is also the fact that any feedback or questions that might come up will not become known by the company management either. Since this kind of feedback is important, if you do go the outside route for training a company manager should be present at every session to listen to what is being said and to offer feedback and direction as well.

You also lose a bit on control over the training sessions as well. Most of the time as in-house trainers go through the training process, they make changes as they go to include new materials that past trainees have asked questions about as well as other things that have made their value known at the sessions proceed. When you hire an outside company to do the sessions they will give the same session over and over again. You might not even have the same trainer gives all the sessions which means that the experience may not be totally uniform or equal.

Train Employees In-House

The second option is to do the training in house with your own managers or employees assuming the role of the trainers. This works extremely well as long as long as you have people who are capable and skilled enough to deliver a quality training session. If you do not have anyone capable of giving training sessions such as these, you might want to look into creating the program and then hiring a trainer to deliver it for you under your supervision.

Keep in mind that not everyone is comfortable or skilled enough to give a training session. The skills required to teach effectively are different than the skills necessary to do a job under normal circumstances. So just because any employee is not capable of training or teaching is not any indication that they are a poor or bad employee as far as the rest of their job is concerned.

Costs of training in-house will chiefly be for materials and the time involved for the employees and trainers to go through the training. There will be no direct outlay of funds for providing the training but there will be loss of productivity for the time allotted for the training. Because of this there should be consideration given to how other work is going to be handled while people are taking the training.

After all you cannot expect someone to train people all day long and still get their regularly assigned work done as well. While this might be able to happen for a day or so, giving many sessions over man days will make it impossible for someone to train and do the rest of their work at the same time. So if a person is designated as a trainer they should have help in getting their normal responsibilities handled while they are training.

The downside of training in-house is that you might not have the right skilled manpower or a sufficient staff to handle the responsibilities of training in conjunction with the rest of their jobs. This is not a little task that can be added to an already full plate. If the trainer is asked or expected to do too much all at one time then the results of everything are bound to suffer.

Because of this careful thought should be made as to whether you have the internals skills and manpower necessary to train in-house. Though the financial savings might be tempting, if you do not have the pieces in place to deliver quality training yourself then the best option might be to hire outside people to do it for you.

Online or Individual Training

The third option is the least desirable option but might be the only choice for certain companies or in certain situations. When we leave training up to the individual to take, we open up a lot of chances for employees refusing or ignoring the training all together. This would be especially true if you are requiring employees to take the training on their own time.

Seminars and online courses as well as books on customer service are all good sources for getting information but the method has a lot of drawbacks. These drawbacks are considerable and you should be aware of them before deciding to let employees do the training on their own.

Customer Service is such a broad term and such a wide subject that it is impossible to just tell someone to go out and learn how to satisfy the customer. That is kind of like telling someone to go out and get you dinner and not telling them what you like to eat.

There would be endless possibilities of what they could bring you back and you might or might lot like what you get. The chances of getting exactly what you would like, including sides and beverage, are almost nil.

If you are going to allow people to take the training individually and on their own schedule, there are a few things you need to be aware of so that you can be reasonably certain people will actually take the training and take it on time.

Here are a few of those things you need to be very explicit about:

The Type of Training

If you want people to take training on their own you need to be specific about which courses, which books or which online or downloaded videos you want them to learn from. Do NOT leave it up to the individual employee for two reasons.

First, there will always be employees who will look for the shortest course, video or book or the one that is the easiest so they can get through the training with a minimal amount of effort. So in those cases, quality takes a back seat to ease and comfort.

Second, when everyone gets to choose which training to take the result is that different people are going to learn different things and different ways of looking at the same thing. When this happen quality flies right out the window and that uniform level of customer service we have talked about so often flies out with it.

So be clear and very specific about what type of training and which course, book or video they are supposed to learn from. Otherwise there could be a wide disparity between the training each employee receives. This will result in different people attacking different problems in different ways and customer satisfaction will suffer as a result.

When to Take the Training

It is important that all employees are ready at the same time when it comes to initiating any kind of change. Otherwise some employees will be prepared while others will not. When this happens the chances of implementing any kind of change successfully are drastically reduced. Because getting the best results is our end goal, we must put deadlines in place whenever possible.

There will be some employees who will take the training or at least schedule it as soon as they are asked.

This is especially true if the training involves anything they see a reason or purpose behind. These are the people who just like to get things done and leave nothing until the last minute.

But there will also be employees who will put this off as long as possible in the hopes that they will not have to take the training at all. These folks hope that management will just forget about it when something else comes along. Or they feel that they might be able to fake their way through things without ever taking the training.

Because everyone is different we will need to set some guidelines and deadlines for every employee as far as when they have to complete each stage of the training. If there is a specific order in which the training should be taken that should be given as well so every person gets the training in the order it is intended to be taken.

Assigning a schedule or deadline will help everyone get the training that they need to be prepared for every step of the process. This will also help provide a more uniform customer experience as everyone will have the same training and viewpoints at each part of the process.

Confirming Training was Actually Taken

Unfortunately there will always be a few people that you cannot trust when it comes to having to do something. So when it comes to training we will need something from the employees to indicate that they did take the training or complete a course by a certain deadline.

Usually this is not a problem because you will have a certificate of completion or some certificate or other form of recognition that is issued when someone leaves the seminar. But in some cases, like with an online course or webinar, there might not be any completion certificate or any other paperwork to prove someone took the course. You cannot use a purchase receipt because even if someone bought a book or paid for a seminar does not mean that they actually watched the webinar or attended the seminar.

In these cases one way to see if people actually took the training is for someone within the company to create a short test or exam with questions designed to test the employee's knowledge of what was covered in that particular training session. If they pass the test at least they know the material. While this doesn't prove they actually took the course, it does show some level of understanding of the subject.

Another benefit of confirming someone took the training is just the requirement to confirm might be enough to get some employees to attend the training. They might be so afraid of not taking the training and being discovered that they will take it just to show they took it. This is not ideal but even sitting in the room or watching the video is bound to teach the individual something.

Ask for Feedback

Regardless what method or type of training you are providing to your company, it is important to provide an easy way for everyone to ask questions and provide feedback. This is especially true at the beginning of the training where feedback can be used to alter future sessions to address more topics or answer specific questions that come up repeatedly.

Feedback is critical because no one understands how things really are when it comes to customers than the people who serve and interact with them every day. Those are the people that can provide valuable insight into what really matter and what the problems really are.

Feedback can be achieved through question and answer sessions, an after class survey or questionnaire and by the instructor involving the trainees in the process by asking them questions and soliciting their answers. The more interactive and engaged everyone is in the class the more knowledge will be obtained by everyone involved.

Customer service training is not designed to be a lecture type format where only the instructor talks. There should be interaction between everyone and role playing and discussions as part of the training. This is the only way everyone can learn everything they need to become customer focused.

Do it Once and Do it Right!

All the steps that we discussed are important for many reasons. Put together, all of these steps will help you identify the most urgent and important needs as well as other areas for improvement. You must not head further into this exercise without a specific sense of direction. To do that will almost guarantee a training program that is lacking in providing everything your employees will need to know to transform your company into a customer focused operation.

Do not rush through any of the steps either thinking they are not important to your company or your situation because they really are.

You cannot make informed decisions without data and information and you cannot create a detailed program without a clear objective. Allow each step to run its course and do not rush the process.

The whole idea at this point is to go through the exercise once and create the program and training system right the first time. Small changes are usually necessary and the entire program will be tweaked and updated over time but the basic structure of the program should be designed correctly the first time.

This is because people do not like change and do not function well in a constantly changing environment. They will embrace change when they see a need or reason behind it but even in those situations if they see changes constantly being made they will question the need for the change and the direction things are headed.

In other words, we are searching for employee buy-in and support and we can only get that if they have confidence in what we are doing and how we are doing it. If we do not do things right before the program is released to the employees then our credibility will be damaged and might never be totally restored no matter how well we do moving forward.

Program Creation

For simplicity sake, we are not going to go through all the details of creating any kind of initiative or program because there are so many variable and so many different approaches, only the individuals or companies involved can make those decisions. With that in mind, however, we would like to go over a few aspects of program creation that will affect the success of your customer service training program.

Here are a few things you need to consider when developing your training program. While not all may apply, it is very likely that most of the following will have at least some impact on your program. So please evaluate each item carefully and take it into consideration and you develop and design your program.

Make it EASY!

Let's be totally honest here.

The easier something is, the more likely it is that we will actually do it. Even more important, the easier something is the more likely it is that we will KEEP ON doing it! No one likes to struggle or work hard to complete something.

The more difficult something is the fewer people that are actually going to work through the program to its completion with their full effort. When people have to struggle with anything a certain percentage of people are just going to give up. Even those who manage to stick with it for a while will eventually get burnt out and just quit.

For our purposes in becoming a customer focused COMPANY, we need every employee to take and complete the training so we are all on the same page and so that we all understand how to do things and why we should do it that way. If everyone doesn't complete the training we will have a company where some do things one way and other do it another. This prevents the creation of a uniform customer experience.

Make it Logical

In order for people to embrace something, it has to make sense.

In order for people to learn something, they must be able to learn in an organized manner and the content must be presented in the proper manner so that people can understand it.

The most effective manner of learning is to build skill upon skill upon skill. By that we mean forming a solid foundation of basic skills on top of which we add more enhanced or advanced skills and so on. The end result is that we eventually learn in an organized manner that allows us to learn an entire skill piece by piece where one piece of knowledge is gradually added to another.

Presenting the material in a logical manner also makes it easier to understand and less confusing. You will actually be following an organized "trip" through the learning process that is more of a straight line instead of something that jumps all over the place. This helps things go more smoothly, make more sense and greatly reduce frustration for the students.

Make it Bite Size

Learning anything usually goes much easier when we break down the lessons or content into small "bite-size" pieces that are easy to learn within a relatively short period of time. This helps make learning easier and more efficient in a number of ways.

First it allows the instructor to handle a small bit of information at a time and helps add discussion and demonstrations in more frequently. It also helps break up the session into shorter and more manageable pieces so individual sessions can be shorter.

Shorter sessions make it easier for training to be scheduled within a busy schedule or packed workday. With more compact and bite-sized" lessons, anyone can squeeze in training much easier into their schedule.

This becomes even more important when you expect people to work their training into their normal workday or after hours. With shorter lessons people can fit their training into shorter periods of time such as on the bus or train ride home, during the evening after dinner or on a meal break while at work.

Shorter and more concise lessons just make it easier on both the instructor and student to get the most out of the training. It also has the added benefit or getting rid of a few of the excuses people usually come up with as to why they couldn't do the training on time. After all, if it takes 30 minutes to complete a less, who [possibly could not schedule that into their lives a few times a week?

Make it Relevant

Most people need to see a reason or benefit for doing something. Some people also are not good at taking generic or general information and converting it into something that applied specifically to them. Because of this, the more specific and relevant we can make the material the more the students are going to see how to use it and how to make it more valuable to them and their jobs.

You can make material more relevant by presenting it using specific examples and applications that apply to the students own company or function. Whenever possible, use your company's own structure and people as examples on how things should be done. You can even use examples of customer service success and failures in the past and why they were handled correctly or how another way could have made them turn out better.

Relevant content helps people get more engaged and remain more engaged throughout the process. It also shows them that there are reasons and applications for what they are learning. This helps make the content appear more valuable and worthwhile to the students. The result is that they will pay closer attention and be more motivated to learn and will remain that way for a longer period of time.

Another benefit is that relevant content helps reduce confusion and misunderstanding by providing specific examples of what certain content is and how it should be used in the company. This way employees get first hand examples to show them how to take what they have just learned and use it in the way the company wants them to use it. This can be extremely powerful when it comes to learning the right way to use the materials they have just learned.

Make it Interactive

When we read what is on the screen or listen to what the instructor is saying we are using just one or two of our senses. While that may be enough to learn the materials being taught, we will get better retention and a higher level of understanding if we engage more senses. One very powerful way of doing this is by making sessions interactive.

That means asking questions designed to produce in-depth answers and the use of exercises such as role playing. By doing this we make people think about the materials and how to apply it. This gets a lot more of our brains engaged.

Take asking questions for example. In order to answer a question, the student has to digest the material, attempt to understand it and then look at the materials in the way the question is designed for them to look at it. Then, the brain has to decide how to answer the question, choose the right words to convey what the student wants to say and then we need to speak those words. That is a LOT of ways to process what we have just learned. This will increase retention and our level of understanding.

Role playing gets us even more involved as we listen to what the other person is saying and then constantly evaluated what we are hearing and how to respond. Even those watching are doing the same thing whether they are aware of it or not. Seeing, speaking, thinking and physical movement are all ways to learn and retain material and information better and longer.

If you are going the self-training route where people take the training on their own through books, make every effort to have content in video form as well so the person is just not reading in the book. Though reading is still a powerful method of learning for most people, having them watch a video will make it even better because it gets more senses involved in the learning process.

Make it Fun

If we make something fun to do, more people will do it. If we make something fun and enjoyable, people will do it longer as well. Plus, they will look forward to the training and form a more positive and accepting feeling about it. If something is viewed as a chore or we feel it is boring or makes us feel uncomfortable, we will tend to make excuses for avoiding it either in part or all together.

Highlight Benefits

It's no secret that if you want someone to get involved with something or to feel excited about it, you need to show them how they will benefit by it. This is the underlying philosophy behind the selling of any product or service. Show them the product and tell them how it will help them make their lives better, easier or more productive. If you convince them of all three, you have a winner of a product.

In the case customer service training, you want to concentrate on how this training is going to make it easier for them to interact with customers and how that will relate into less stress, easier workdays and higher productivity. For most people, the "less stress" part will be enough to get their initial buy in.

Try and have a featured benefit for every lesson or concept that you have in our course or program. We need to constantly reinforce that there are real benefits for the student in taking this course and applying this information. This will help them get engaged, remain engaged and provide their best efforts.

Make it Convenient

For many people, convenience is an important component of everything they purchase or do in life. If you can make something more convenient to get to or to use, you will have more people interested in using or taking it.

Making your program more convenient might mean changing the hours when classes are given or holding several sessions and letting employees pick the best ones for their schedules. If the training is given off-site it might mean making the location as convenient and easy to get to as possible for most of the employees.

As far as the length of time each session takes that can be important as well as some employees might not have the time to take a single 8 hours class and might find 2 - 4hour classes or even 4 - 2 hours classes preferable. Of course it is not possible to please every employee all the time but at least consider this when you are designing your training program.

Provide Resource Materials

Some of the most beneficial learning often comes after the training session is over. It occurs when the employee starts taking what they have learned and starts implementing it. But sometimes they have questions or are unsure about what to do and how to go about doing it. After all, we all do not remember every little bit of information we were taught. The longer period of time between when we learned and when we start using the knowledge the more of the little things we forget.

Because of this having some reference materials, such as a workbook or course handbook, can come in very handy. Employees can go back and refresh their memory by re-reading the content or they can just refer back to things when the need arises. This will enable the employee to get information faster than having to find someone to ask.

Sometimes it is also beneficial to furnish a book or e-book on the same subject of the training so they can use that as a resource as well. Sometimes this works especially well because the employee gets to read things from another author and can get a different view of the same content.

Whatever format you decide, it is always a good idea to give the employee something to take home with them at the end of the session.

Workbooks always work well because these workbooks also give them a place to write any notes they made during the course of the session. So when they go back to read the content again their notes are all in the same place.

Create Workplace Mentors & Tutors

Because of the learning curve there will always be a need for people in the workplace to act as mentors or advisors to the employees. In some cases these mentors could be the employee's managers or supervisors. Or they could be designated people who have been trained to function in that position.

Whoever these people might be, they would be the individuals to provide on the job support and follow-up training as needed to anyone who needs or requests it. This is a valuable position and the people assigned to it should be chosen carefully. This is because they will instruct your employees on how they should do things and you want their instructions to be clear, concise and accurate.

Since some employees might be reluctant or embarrassed to ask for help. These mentors or tutors should be in a position to observe as well as mentor. That means they should be positioned in such a way that they can easily see how your employees are functioning in their daily jobs.

By being able to observe how employees are actually interacting with the customers and performing their daily duties, they will be in a better position to see where assistance and guidance is needed and will be able to function pro-actively instead of reactively.

This means that they will not have to wait until employees come to them but instead they will be able to spot problems or areas of improvement earlier, step in and get things moving in the right direction much earlier and faster.

Make it Adaptable for New Employees

Any well designed program should also be able to handle new employees as they enter the company. This will always be the case because you will have people leave for other jobs, retire, let go for other reasons and hopefully be needed for expansion as your workforce increases. Regardless of the reason these new employees come into the company they will still need to be trained on the same concepts that your current employees are being trained on now.

Training new employees can pose a problem because they usually will not enter the company in groups large enough to hold a training class.

Unless you are having an expansion hiring, new employees might come in one or two at a time. Because of this it could take months or longer to have enough for a training class. We cannot afford to wait that long.

Because of this we need to develop course materials that will be enough to get these new employees training on the basics until there is a full training class started in the future. These materials should be in the form of self-study handbooks, manuals and training videos. You might even schedule time during their first week or two on the job to take this short form of training. Make it part of their introductory period.

New employees could also be assigned to a mentor that would help them understand the company's customer focused environment and help them implement the same techniques and attitudes that existing employees already have. This will enable the new employees to get on board and fit in much faster than if they had to wait for a group session.

Then, as the number of new employees increases a new training class can be started and the formal training can begin.

Have Additional Training Available

While most of your employees will "get it" from the first round of training, others might not.

Since everyone learns at a different rate and while everyone might not have the same skills or experience going into the training, there will be some employees that might benefit from a second round of training.

This training might be a little bit different and might exist of specific topics chosen by the managers or supervisors of the employees taking the class. This training might focus on areas where these employee are encountering a specific kind of trouble and be designed to provide specific and detailed help.

This is preferable to allowing the employee to continue to struggle and potentially cause problems for other employees and customers. Needing this additional training does not necessarily mean that these employees are not good employees or inferior to others. It just means that they need extra help in learning the material.

You might even offer follow-up training on specific topics and open it up to anyone who feels they have a real need for that particular training. That way people who feel a little uncomfortable with certain techniques can get additional training to help them function at a higher level. This works well because there will always be people who look like they get it on the outside but are struggling on the inside.

Summary

Hopefully now you see some of the important aspects of program creation and how they might make it easier for your employees while still producing excellent results. Doing well within a program is not always an easy task and if there are things we can do to allow more people to learn at a higher level then everyone benefits.

So as you go through the design and creation of your customer focused program keep all of these things in mind and integrate as many of them as possible into the program. Your employees will benefit and so will the company.

The Roll Out

Now we have created our program, hopefully done a bit of "debugging" and tweaking and finally have it ready for a company-wide rollout. If you haven't tested the program out on a few chosen employees or management, then now would be an excellent time to do so. That way you can get even more feedback and have one last chance to remove any problems or bugs in the program before the employee see it.

Keep in mind that you basically have one chance to get this program into the hands of employees and experience the greatest chance of success. If you do this wrong, you will be able to go back and make changes but it is likely that you will lose a few employees in the process and make a few other skeptical as well. So let's all agree that it makes sense to take some time to roll out the program right.

Here are a few things to consider as you figure out how to take your new program or initiative and get it out into the hands of the employees:

Don't Rush the Rollout

Anything worth doing is worth doing right so don't try and get the roll-out done too fast. Unless there are specific and urgent needs that have to be addressed, you have time to do it right. So take your time and prepare yourself well for what lies ahead.

Explain the Reasons Behind It

Every rule, procedure or change has some background behind it. In other words, there are specific reasons for wanting or needing to undertake these changes. Don't think your employees understand all of this because they might not. So let's not take any chances and make sure they know why we are doing what we are doing.

The reason for this is that most people will get behind something if they see the reasons behind it. If these changes will make the company better or more secure, people will get behind it. If it will create more jobs and more advancement opportunities, your employees will support it.

Remember that some of your employees only see the part of the business that they are involved in. They might be totally unaware of what is going on in the rest of the company. So taking a bit of time at the start letting everyone know and understand why all of this is necessary will help more employees get behind the program and give their best efforts.

Share the Goals Ahead

Contrary to what some managers might think, most employees need to see the "big picture". They need to see how their efforts contribute to the overall success of the company. In other words, they need to feel part of the family and understand that what they do and how they do it has value. People need to feel important and taking the time to share the goals and challenges ahead brings employees closer to the company.

It is also important that employees understand the goals ahead because understanding the goal makes it easier to see the value or reason behind what they are being asked to do. For example, if higher customer satisfaction leads to increased sales and they know that one of the company goals for the next year is to increase sales by 10%, they will see a need to make customers happier and increase customer satisfaction.

Most employees will not follow many things blindly just because they are told to. Some will because the need their jobs but even those employees are not likely to give their best efforts to something they don't see the value in. So if you want employees to give their best efforts, then spend the time to share goals and objectives with all your employees.

Detail the Benefits to the Company and the Employees

We have already discussed this but this is so critical to the roll-out that we need to go over this again. People always respond better to things that will benefit them personally in their lives. If you can show them how they will benefit by getting behind this program then they will be far more likely to give a better effort.

For example, if you tell an employee that they have to do something because the company needs to increase sales by 10%, they are not likely to get too excited about that. But if you tell them that increasing sales by 10% will help avoid a reduction in the workforce or enable them to increase profit sharing or will increase employee advancement and higher salaries, you will most certainly have gotten their attention!

Also, do not leave it up to the employee to figure out how something is going to benefit them. Lead them step by step through the program and point out every single way you know of that supporting this program will benefit the employees. Don't hold anything back because sometimes even the smallest benefit might mean a whole lot to a few particular employees.

Make the Roll Out Manageable for Everyone

Changes almost always require learning, sacrifice and a period of adjustment. Because of this some employees are going to view this as an inconvenience and a disruption. To minimize these feelings, make the roll-out as easy and manageable as you can for the employees.

This means giving them enough time to take the training without causing a major issue with the rest of their workday or personal life. It means keeping change to a minimum and making sure the employees are supported throughout the program. If you don't ask for or expect too much, too soon your employees will appreciate that and come to realize that this is not all that big of a deal.

Consider the Impact on Employees

Before rolling out any program, take one last important step and consider how this particular program of change is going to impact the employee. Survey the department managers or even ask a few trusted employees for their input on how this will impact the employees.

Then, as you get this data, try and figure out ways to address every concern or objection by making things easier or making certain concessions. This does not mean you need to abandon anything in entirety because your employees say it is too much. But it does mean you can try and make things as easy as possible so that you can get a higher degree of acceptance from those same employees.

Creating Gradual Improvement

Some companies, and some people think that as soon as a person or company becomes trained then everything falls into line immediately and all problems simply go away leading to peace and tranquility. If you are one of those people, it is time that you woke up and inhale a little bit of reality.

Even the most powerful race car does not go from 0 to 200 miles an hour instantaneously. There is a time when it has to build up speed before everything is working at its best. The same must happen whenever a company decides to make a commitment to become customer focused. It is not like turning on a switch and the lights go on at full brightness. Instead, it is like using a dimmer to go from darkness to full brightness.

It is going to take time for everything to fall into place.

Just like it takes time for a new employee to learn their job or for an existing employee to learn a new skill so will it take time to take what they have just learned in training and be able to use it in their daily activities.

Training is a practical exercise where theory and knowledge are given to a student. It is then up to the student to take that practical knowledge and turn it into some form of reality. As the employee starts to do this, he or she will go through 3 stages of performance.

Stage One – Learning to Apply

In stage one, the employee or trainee attempts to take what they have just learned and turn it into a practical application in their daily routine. At first this application will be slow and even a bit awkward as the person works slowly through the process. Their application as this point is not fluid and not polished. It will take them longer to do something and they will get less than optimal results as well. But this is something that everyone goes through.

During this phase there will be many questions or a lot of consulting back to the training materials. There will be a good deal of uncertainty as people trying to do something for the first time are unsure if they are doing it the right way. So there will be a lot of hesitation and second guessing as well.

During this time we will be constantly changing our approach and thought process to become more polished and more adept at what we are doing. We will gradually understand what we are doing wrong or what we can do better and we will constantly be improving our performance and getting better results.

The better the training and the more practical exercises and role playing the trainee goes through the more prepared and confident they will be earlier in the process. That is why the quality of training is so important when it comes to getting the best results in the shortest period of time.

Stage Two – Conscious Application

Stage two is where we reach a point where we are fairly proficient in what we are doing and have addressed most, if not all, of the problems in our approach and delivery. We do more things right and do them with more ease and more polish. We know what we need to do and we concentrate on what we are doing and what has been proven to work for us.

In other words, we know what to do, we know how to do it and we just have to think about what the situation is to understand what needs to be done. We are getting more efficient and requiring less time to handle almost every situation.

We are functioning at a higher level and our customers are noticing better improvement from your employees.

This stage can take a fairly long time to work through. Some people may "get it" right away while others might have to spend significant time working through the process and become comfortable with it. There is no one perfect or normal time frame. You must allow people to work through things at their own pace until they become comfortable with it.

Stage Three – Application Become a Habit

This is the stage that we eventually want every employee to get to. At this stage we do things automatically without needing to stop and think about what needs to be done. We just allow our brains to process everything behind the scenes and tell us what to do.

People who reach this stage instinctively understand what to do and also what not to do. They know which words to use and when to use them. Their minds are constantly looking, watching observing and processing information so that they will make the best and most accurate decisions that vast majority of the time.

This is where people function at their highest level and obtain their greatest level of performance.

They accomplish much more in less time and make fewer mistakes. They can recognize trouble early in the process and therefore resolve problems earlier when they are easier and less costly to resolve. Even more important, people at this stage are the ones that other employees look to for help and information so that they too can reach this level.

As people go through these stages, they will take the information they learned during training and add to that information their personal experiences and job specific knowledge they already had into the process. The more they can combine practical training with real-life experience the faster they will proceed through all the stages.

One common mistake that is frequently made after training is the pressure from management to go through these steps as quickly as possible. Because there were costs involved in providing this training, the company wants or even demands to see results almost immediately. But sometimes those results do not show up immediately in reports or behavior. Even when they do the changes in to customer attitudes may be subtle.

That is not to say that management or any individual must be patient forever.

Individuals can understand when they are giving their best efforts and they know what they need to do in order to learn what they need to learn and how to implement it.

But management cannot have that kind of insight into the minds of each employee so in those cases we need to establish a reasonable base line for how well employees are doing in implementing their new found knowledge. This baseline will depend on how most of your employees are performing at various times after training.

For example, if you train 100 people and 75 of them are able to apply the information and techniques they learned within 6 months of taking the training, you might be reasonable expecting the majority of your employees to be reasonably functional within 6 months. Some might get it earlier and some might take a little bit longer. But that 6 month time frame is when you would like people to be reasonably functional.

So if Bob and Lou take the training and in 5 months Lou is doing great but Bob still is helplessly lost, you might have legitimate concerns about whether Bob will ever "get it". Bob might need some update or refresher training to help him get onboard.

Which bring us to our last item in getting results:

Update or Refresher Training

One of the most common misconceptions when it comes to customer service training is that once you are trained that's it. There is no need for any further training. After all, customer service training is all about communication and understanding so what else could you possibly learn after you are trained?

Well, refresher or update training enables people to build upon their previous skills to form an even greater or in-depth level of understanding. If you stop and think about it, when we were trained the first time we had little experience or knowledge to build upon. We had a few pieces but we couldn't really put them all together to make much sense of them.

So we worked to adapt the knowledge to our particular job or situation. We took the pieces of what we learned and put them together so they made sense to us and what we are doing. In other words, we turned generic knowledge into targeted job specific information that had much more relevance than what we heard from the trainer or read in the book.

So now that we have the solid base of skills and knowledge we can now approach advanced knowledge and understand why this knowledge is so important and how we can use it to make our jobs easier and better all at the same time. What happens now is that our basic understanding gives us the ability to learn even more and become even more focused.

We should never become complacent once we have become committed to customer service. Our competitors are always looking for ways to steal our customers from us and we must take every step possible to make that as difficult for them as possible.

Additional training on a scheduled basis will not only tell our employees that customer service is still appropriately for the company but it will also give the employees the tools and resources they need to take their performance and understanding to higher levels. This can only result in higher customer care and higher customer satisfaction.

Making it Easy to Contribute

Throughout the evaluation, design and implementation phases of the process, various people at all levels within the company might have useful input that will help make the process go faster, become easier and at the same be more accurate and focused. The problem is that sometimes companies do not make it very easy for these employees to share their thoughts and ideas with the people who are responsible for the training.

It would be foolish to not take advantage of the knowledge and wisdom that can only come by actually living through the business on a daily basis. Direct interaction with the customers gives some employees first-hand experience of what our customers want, what their needs are and what they like or dislike about our business.

In some companies management thinks that they alone are the best judges of what the company needs to move forward and they might even be right. But that still doesn't mean that the input of all employees might not have real value throughout the process. To dismiss the input of someone because they are not a manager is both short-sighted and downright foolish.

The best way or getting everyone to share their knowledge and experience is to make it extremely easy for them to do so. In most cases this requires management approaching the employees and soliciting this information. In other words, don't wait for the employees to speak up. Ask them what they think and what they might have to add.

It might even be a great idea to have one or two of the employees who have daily direct contact with customers to be part of your project design team. This would give them an almost unlimited opportunity to speak their mind and provide their perspective on how we need to move forward and become more customer focused.

People also tend to look at things differently. So what might not bother one person might really anger another person. What works well for some employees might not work for others. Different perspectives as well as different job responsibilities gives our employees a unique perspective on what is going on out there between our customers and our company.

The other reason for including everyone in the process is that sometimes people removed from the process create what they believe is the very best rule, policy or procedure but when it gets down to the people who actually are charged with implementing it, it is made abundantly clear that there are many reasons why it just will not work!

There are many instances where something looks great on paper but fails miserably when it is actually implanted. There is a place for real world, practical experience when it comes to creating new programs, rules and policies.

If you are not comfortable with having certain employees as part of the project design team, then at least bring several employees in after the program has been designed and run everything by them first and ask for their input. It is much better and cheaper that we discover potential problems now instead of rolling out the entire program to everyone and finding out then that there are real problems with it.

It should be mentioned now that soliciting input from employees must be done carefully and honestly. You must encourage people to be totally honest and not just make them feel they can only say what they feel you want to hear.

You want people to speak up when they think that something is wrong or will not work. You do not want to instill fear if people say something you do not want to hear.

Because some people will feel intimidated no matter how much you tell them to be honest, sometimes it is best to allow people to submit their comments and thoughts anonymously. This way people ca be honest and not have to worry about their comments and criticism coming back on them. A perfect example of anonymous reporting might be a suggestion box where people can drop their comments without having their name on the paper.

Whenever you receive a comment, treat it with respect and give it a chance in your head before you immediately dismiss it because it is somewhat negative in nature. People who design a product or a program tend to take criticism personally and when this takes place good and important comments sometimes just get thrown away or dismissed.

I recommend that at least two or three people each look at each comment. If any one of the three people feel that a common has merit, it should be brought to management for discussion. This lessens the number of times one person might take something that has merit and dismiss it because they thought it was personal in nature.

Just because someone submits a comment does not mean it has to be acted upon. Some comments will be without merit and some might indeed be personal attacks made with a personal agenda behind them. So have the comments screened by two or three people and only act or discus the ones that appear to have merit. File the others away for future use if needed.

Even if a comment does not appear to have merit, keep it for a while to see if similar, or even the same, comments come in from more than one person. The same comment submitted over and over by different people might indicate that it does have merit because several people experienced that same issue or problem. Remember we are looking for what our customers feel are problems and issues so what they express to our employees does matter. It makes no difference if we think something is just fine the way it is if it angers or upsets our customers!

Last, but certainly not least in some cases, consider running some kind of contest where the top suggestions winds some kind of prize. This is just another incentive to get people to share what is on their mind. The more people who share the more information you get. The more information you get the better informed you will be and the better your decisions will be as well!

Reports, Data and Feedback

We already talked about the need for reports and data in the very beginning to make sure we have correctly identified all the problems or objectives that we need to address before we start creating our training program. This is important regardless of who is creating the program. Trying to design an effective program without knowing the problems or needs involved is almost impossible.

But data and reports and feedback are also required throughout the design phase and during the implementation of the program at all levels. Without this information we may never know if what we are doing is working well, somewhat working or not working at all. We need feedback and we need follow-up.

Sometimes we think that we have covered all the bases, correctly uncovered all the facts and all the goals and have pretty much done a great job in designing the program.

Then we felt that we rolled it out in the right manner to help insure that we get the best results possible. In other words, we think we have done our best and that everything that should have been done has been done and been done correctly.

While that might be true, things have been known to go very wrong even with the best intentions and the most in-depth preparation. People are funny at times and they reaction we expect might not be the reaction we get. Because of this, we need to make sure what we want or need to see happen is, in fact, happening.

This can be different when it comes to customer service because you may not see a dramatic rise in sales like you might with a new sales promotion and you might not see a difference in reported problems either. In fact, it could be months before you notice any changes that have come from your efforts! And even those might not be measurable!

Because of this we need to survey or poll the employees to get their input on how things are going. We can even do a phone or exit poll of our customers to get an idea of how they feel. Customer polls are even more useful if we had done a few polls before we made the changes to get something to compare the results to.

But if we do not have that luxury we can ask questions designed to compare the level of customer service they received now to the level of service they received at some point in the past.

Even the best programs often require small corrections designed to address unexpected issues or problems that may arise. These little corrections are usually nothing overly involved or costly but they are necessary to keep things moving in the right direction and continually striving to get the best results possible.

Depending on the size of your company and the amount of changes you have made, you will probably want to keep track of things over the course of the next year or so to get an idea of both long and short term results. It might take that long for customers to be impressed and start recommending your company to other people. Because of this sales might not increase for several months or even a year or more. But that does not mean that your efforts are not working.

I would run polls or gather information at least quarterly to start. If your business has accounting periods then perhaps you might want to gather data every period so that you are better able to spot trends and other information.

Keep in mind that the more often you gather data the earlier you will become aware of problems that have popped up or corrective action that is needed. The faster you take action the lower the impact will be on your company and your customers.

You also need to be careful to measure equivalent data when you compare time frames and performance. Some industries or businesses have difference levels of sales at different times of the year so for comparisons to be accurate and valid, you need to compare data from the same time periods or time of year.

It may surprise you but customer problems can be seasonal as well. Usually problems are a reflection of sales so as sales increase, problems usually increase as well. Sometimes problems will lag sales a bit so you need to take that into consideration as well. So if you are doing a comparison between today and the past, pick the same time of year and make sure you factor the amount of sales into calculating whether the number of customer issues or problems has risen or remained flat as well.

For example, if you did $1,000,000 in sales last year and had 500 customer problems, and this year, after your changes you did $3,000,000 and had 1,000 customer problems, you might think that customer problems increased and things were not working well. But when you fact in the fact that sales actually grew 300% over the year but problems grew just 200% you can actually see a positive trend starting from your efforts.

I should also mention that so much of customer service cannot be accurately measured or described with numbers on a sales chart or a spreadsheet. So much of customer service is based on emotion and perception that we really cannot put an accurate number on what our customers are going to do if they are more satisfied now than they were last year. We have no idea whether they will tell 10 people or 1,000 people about how pleased they were with us.

Because of this, a significant portion of our feedback is going to come from our employees who will see first-hand how our customers are feeling towards us. If things are going well they might report less stress and easier problem resolution. They might report an increase in positive comments from customers and relay personal stories about how some new policy or approach paid off with one particular customer.

This is the information that you are going to need in order to reassure yourself and confirm that your efforts are still heading in the right direction. This is not something you can just decide is working. Though your gut instinct will often point you in the right direction it is also good to get actual hard confirmation that you are doing the right things most of the time.

This information can let you know when it is time for additional or follow-up training or when it might be time to take everything to the next level because your customers responded so well to your first round of changes. Whatever you use the information you gather, it is important that you make the effort to gather this information, analyze it and apply it properly so you can get the most from your efforts.

Even after the training is completed, you are still going to want to run surveys and polls to make sure your efforts are being sustained and that people are not falling back into old habits. Or, even more common that your competition has noticed your growth and has now stepped up their game so your company no longer has the same advantages that it once had.

You do not have to follow up as often as you did in the beginning but you still need to gauge the feelings of your customers at least once a year. Two or three times might be better.

After all, it couldn't hurt!

Roadblocks & How to Avoid Them

Ok, even the best intentioned people who put their best efforts into the project will tell you that there are always things that get in the way. Also, sometimes what the mind dreams the wallet cannot produce. Which means that sometimes we need to compromise when we do not have the funds or resources to do exactly what we wanted to do in the first place.

This chapter is going to discuss a few common problems or roadblocks that can keep us from reaching our objectives or getting the best results. You might not encounter any or all of these but it is a good idea to understand them so you will not be caught off guard when one of them pops up in your life!

Here are a few of the most common roadblocks when it comes to becoming Customer Focused:

A Poorly Designed Program

A poorly designed or rolled out program does not inspire the confidence of the employees. When employees see something they are not impressed with or feel will address the core problems or goals, they will not stand behind it or give it their best effort.

In fact, some employees might see a poorly designed program as a lack of commitment or a lack of proper thought by management. When these kinds of feeling surface, people question why more time, thought and effort did not go into the creation of a good program. Then they figure if it wasn't worth the efforts of management then it shouldn't be worth their efforts either.

You can eliminate this by going through the steps we outlined and by taking your time to do each step correctly. Unless there are serious problems that require immediate and drastic action, there is no reward for rushing the new program out to employees. It is better to work out the kinks and problems early in the process and then reveal a well-designed and polished program out to the employees. This will inspire confidence and commitment from your employees.

Lack of Focus

When you start trying to become more customer focused, that should be your goal.

It should be your primary objective. But sometimes people add things to the program that really aren't related to becoming customer focused. Instead of one objective we now have 47 objectives with each one pulling us in different directions and taking away part of our attention and focus.

There is nothing wrong with developing a multi-phase program where you start with the basics and then, over time, add different skill sets and focus points to the original training. In fact, that is exactly the way good organizations and committed people approach their training. Pick one objective and then focus on that objective until you achieve it. Then move on to other skills that you can add to your current ones.

But when you take that one objective and add so much into it that it dilutes the original objective just confuses and frustrates people. People need to see and understand a clear vision in order to convince themselves that all of this is worth their effort. They need to see that management is focused on something before they can focus on the same thing. If management is changing their minds every other day the employees will do that as well.

Thinking that Customer Service is Black & White

Some companies and individuals think that customer service is a black and white issue. By that we mean that there is just one way to make a customer happy and that it should be easy to know what to do in every situation as long as you are sufficiently trained.

The reality is that customer service is more "gray area" than black and white. Since every situation is different and every customer is different as well, it is virtually impossible to create a "one size fits all" resolution for every situation.

Customer Service requires a lot of investigation and analysis. It requires that we look at the customer and the situation and try and decide among several possible resolutions or steps to try and make that customer happy. At any time we might make the wrong decision or the customer might react in unexpected ways and the situation will either get worse or remain unresolved.

This type of situation is part training and part experience. Once people learn the basics it is up to them to develop their approach and skill sets over time and become more proficient when it comes to interacting with the customer. Thinking that everything should be black and white is one viewpoint that should be kicked out the door immediately. THAT is one thing that is black & white!

Expecting or Demanding Too Much Too Soon

Training anyone on anything new is a process and customer service training is no different. It is going to take time for people to learn the material and figure out how to implement it in their job and approach to the customer. You do not just turn a switch and go to instant perfection overnight.

Many times management at one level have expectations that are just unreasonable. These expectations add pressure on the people who are taking the training and trying to learn the material and the pressure makes it more difficult for them to practice what they have learned. It also creates an atmosphere that is difficult to work in.

Also keep in mind that it can take several great experiences to change the attitude of the customer after just one bad experience. So the changes you made might be paying huge benefits that you just can't see yet. Customers are pleased with the new direction but remain skeptical. Over time, as they see that this is really the way they are going to be treated from now on, they will start doing more business and telling more people. THEN and only then, will you see the benefits in your bottom line.

Work out a time line of what you honestly would like to see happen and by what date. Make this reasonable and achievable so there will not be too much pressure and frustration for any manager or employee.

Too Little Patience

As people learn new things or try to develop new skills, mistakes will be made and we have to be patient with them. Implementing training is a learning process and whenever there are decisions to be made and options to consider, people will on occasion make the wrong calls. Even the best employee or the most skilled manager will make mistakes.

We need to take those mistakes and turn them into learning experiences instead. Go over what happened with the employee, or even with the entire group, and show them your thought process and what the company would like to see happen in the future when the same or similar situation comes up again.

In the beginning there will be a lot of mistakes as people get used to the new processes and the new approach to customer service. But as employees make mistakes and as those mistakes are used to teach others, these mistakes will happen less and less frequently over time. They will never totally go away as judgment calls will always come into play and new employees will make their own mistakes. But they should level out to a very small number relatively shortly.

Lack of "Buy-In" from Employees

In order for any change to be successful, everyone involved in the change must support it and work hard to make it a success. But sometimes we don't get the support from the employees for any number of reasons. This will make it a lot more difficult to get the results we want in the time frame we need.

The most common reasons for lack of "buy in" is that the employees feel that this is just another initiative that will soon pass and that there is no need for them to invest their time or energy in it. This attitude usually comes from their experience when in the past the company has changed their approach and focus so often that no one has any faith in what the company is doing.

Another reason is that the employees might not support or agree with the new initiative or changes and whenever we don't agree with something, we often give it less than our best effort.

To combat this attitude and problem we need to take special care to design the right program and do it for the right reasons. It should focus on real problems and provide a benefit for the company and the employees.

When we have done this we need to "sell" the program to the employees in such a way that they become excited because they see the benefits for them in doing what the company wants.

When you release the program to the employees, lead them through all the benefits that the program will bring to THEM. Show them how they will have less stress, a more pleasant work environment and other benefits that they will see if they just follow the program. When people see personal benefits in doing something they will usually give a better and more sustained effort.

You can address many of the causes of employee non-engagement through careful program design, proper roll out and carefully presenting the program to everyone. Doing this in the right way will increase engagement and provide better results over a longer period of time.

Not Enough Resources

Sometimes intentions are good and everything else is ready to go but there are just not enough resources to do what you want and how you want to do it. This is true for both companies and individuals. When this happens you have a couple of decisions to make.

First and foremost, ask yourself if there are any critical issues or problems that need to be addressed. If there are, perhaps you can create a smaller scale program to address just those issues. That might require less resources and enable you to address your short term needs.

If there are no immediate needs or problems then perhaps consider designing a tiered program where you gradually implement various levels of training over longer periods of time. For example you might consider training people with a short course in customer service basics just to get things started. Then, as more resources become available you can continue training everyone in more advanced or specific skills.

One option you should try to stay away with is training just some people in the company first and then training the rest later. While this might be an option for your company, there is one very real and important downside to this approach. That would be that some people in your company will want to do things the new way while the untrained people will want to do things the old way. This can lead to confusion, frustration and prevent you from creating the uniform customer experience that we have been talking about throughout this book.

You can also investigate the various training options available to you for various parts of the training. To save money maybe you have everyone learn the basics through reading a company provided book. Then the advanced training can take place and be taught by a live training session with a trainer.

There are many options when it comes to training and some will be less expensive than others. Be sure to investigate all of them and come up with the best option for you. And remember that one option can be used for one part of the training while another option is used for other parts. Every company or individual is different and every training program is different as well. Identify the best options and use what works for you.

No One Trained to Become Your Trainer

I have taken a few company sponsored and taught training sessions and let me tell you, one of the worst experiences is being taught by someone who has limited or no skills when it comes to training others. Just knowing the materials or being a good employee does not mean that you are going to be a good trainer.

I strongly suggest that you be very careful when choosing who will be your in-house trainer.

The person should be personable and outgoing without being overbearing or appearing to be superior to the people he or she is training. He should also have a speaking voice and personality that inspires confidence and makes people want to listen. Plus, the person should feel comfortable talking to large groups and be able to control the sessions and keep them on track.

If you do have people on staff that you feel might be good choices, I strongly urge you to send them to a seminar on how to train others. At this seminar they will learn how to structure a session, how to control and lead participants and how to deliver information effectively. You would be surprised how much people can learn about training in one of these programs.

Once you have chosen your trainer(s) have them give their first sessions to management before they actually give a session to the rest of the employees. It is best that they "practice" on those who have created the program so feedback not only on the trainer but on the content as well can take place at that point.

Lack of Proper Modelling by Management

This is potentially one of the most dangerous and deadly roadblocks of them all and it occurs far more frequently than it should. Management develops a program, implements the program to the employees and then fails to follow the rules and objectives of the program. They skirt around new policies and procedures and violate them at will whenever they see the need to do so.

When this happens the employee wonder why one group has to follow the new rules while another doesn't. Then they question whether the new rules are all that important and whether or not they even work. They also feel that if it is easier to work around them for their benefit, why not since others are doing that as well.

I worked at one company where employees were told to handle a particular customer situation one specific way. When an employee did that and the customer got angry and wrote a letter to management, the management yelled and screamed at that employee for following the rule that they instituted! When employees see this type of behavior and attitude they question what they should do in any situation.

In order for employees to follow the rules and embrace the concepts they need to see management do the same. Management needs to set the right example by modelling the right behavior 100% of the time.

In those instances where exceptions must be made, management needs to communicate why those changes were made and the reasons behind them. That way the employees see the reasons behind the behavior and will not question what happened as much as they might have.

Another reason for the explanation is that the situation can be used as a teaching tool so that everyone will understand why those steps were taken and this can influence behavior and decision making in similar situations in the future. This helps both management and the employees understand the process and enable them to make the best decisions and take the most appropriate action every time.

Employee Overload / Burnout

Sometimes people who are asked to do something different or new encounter problems combining these new efforts with an already overloaded schedule. They just don't have the time to take the training and do all the other work that is already on their plate and manage to do all of this within their normal work day.

I worked in one company where I was asked to do something that would take up over 25% of my workweek.

When I asked my manager when I was supposed to do the rest of my work he replied "That's what evenings and weekends are for!" While that might work on a rare or occasional basis, you cannot expect people to put in extra-long hours on a regular basis.

The other part of the process involves stress and time. It takes longer to do the same task or process a new or different way until you become accustomed and comfortable with the new process. During this "get acquainted time" there will be more stress as well because we are doing something we are not comfortable with as yet.

All of this can add up to an overloaded and stressed out staff that just cannot function at an optimum level as much as they might want to. So even if the desire is there, the body and mind will just not be able to keep up.

You can take steps to minimize this by being realistic and honest about the impact that all of these changes are going to have on your employees. There are three main areas that you need to be aware of and concerned about.

The first is the time required to take the training. Ask yourself if your employees are going to be able to take the time required to take the training and still be able to get their regular work done. If they can't perhaps you can add temporary manpower to help get this work completed. Or, if agreeable with the employees, authorize overtime pay to get that work completed.

The second area is the time required to implement the materials learned and be comfortable with it. This is also going to take time and patience on both the employees and management. It might negatively impact some goals or measures but that is to be expected and should be planned for.

The third area is how these changes are going to permanently impact the company and what effects these changes are going to have on your employees. Are the changes going to create more work and more time to get the same tasks done? Are the new processes more time consuming as well?

Any change that requires more time and more effort is going to impact both the company and the employees and might even require changes in manpower. Management needs to be aware of this so that employees are not being overburdened and overworked.

Lack of Commitment

Sometimes when the best efforts are made and the best programs are created, the effort in implementing these programs just isn't there. In other words, employees, and even management, is just not willing to give the time and effort that it will take to result in success. This can occur for several reasons.

Employees might be already overworked and just cannot handle even one more task or project. One more thing might just send them past the breaking point. When this happens employees often just shut down.

In some cases, this is just the latest in changes or programs that employees are just plain tired of having to deal with. If you see an almost universal rejection of the program this could very well be the reason behind the attitude.

It is also possible that lower levels of management are not on board with the program and are not presenting it with the proper attitude or force when it comes to the employees. Employees notice when their managers are not excited about something and you cannot expect someone to get excited about something their boss is not fully behind.

It might also be an employee issue when it comes to just a few people not giving the proper effort or commitment. When this happens you either have to talk with that employee and encourage them to participate. If that works, then great. But if the employee does still not respond properly you might have to reconsider if this employee has the attitudes that you look for in your employees.

Last, but certainly not least, the environment and atmosphere of the company often plays a significant role in how employees respond to new programs and initiatives.

If your employees have a positive attitude towards the company they will usually give a superior effort. But if the company has not treated their employees well or if the employees have a negative attitude towards the company then anything new or different is not likely to be received well by the employees.

The best way to get the highest level of commitment and environment is to create a workplace atmosphere where employees have a positive feeling or attitude towards the company and truly want it to succeed. You want to have employees emotionally invested I the success of the company.

This means making employees feel appreciated, valued and important to the overall success of the company. It means letting them know that their voices and ideas are valued by management and ownership. If you can create this type of feeling with your employees then you will stand a much greater chance of success with this program as well as all others.

Insincerity

When a company does anything with the wrong intent the employees can pick up on this.

For example, if the company embarks on an initiative because it is the currently acceptable thing to do but the company doesn't actually stand behind it, employees will notice.

It is like the CEO telling employee they need to save energy and recycle and protect the environment yet they see him leave all the lights on in his office 24/7 and see him drive to and from work in a huge gas guzzling luxury vehicle. When they see something being done for the wrong reasons, employees will not usually give it their best efforts.

You can avoid this by becoming customer focused for all the right reasons. Don't do it because everyone else is if you don't believe in it. Do it because you see the advantages and because it is good for the company. It is perfectly fine to become customer focused because it will lead to more sales because that is what businesses are always looking for. But don't just say you are going to be customer focused because everyone else is saying it as well.

Initial Problems / Failures

How we handle problems or failures can become a significant stumbling block or roadblock as well. Some people or companies are quick to give up at the first sign of trouble. They abandon something without giving it a real chance to succeed.

The correct thing to do when you encounter a problem or set back is to calmly look at what has occurred and try and figure out why it occurred and how we can change or modify something to help get things back on track. Most of the time, if the proper efforts were made at the very beginning, only minor changes or adjustments will be required to get back on the right track. Rarely will an entire program have to be thrown away and started again from scratch.

Also, large scale changes or panic reduces the level of confidence among the employees in both the program and management's ability to keep things running smoothly. The ability to make minor changes on the fly with the least amount of trouble or panic will create higher confidence in the minds of the employees.

Good companies treat problems and set-backs as learning experiences that help them become more knowledgeable and prepared for the future. This will help keep running at an optimum level and help insure that the good results we see now will continue in the future.

Too Many Changes or Constant Changes

We mentioned more than once throughout this book the need to do things right from the start to minimize the number or degree of changes that might be needed throughout the process. This is important because most people do not like change and can only deal with so much of it. After that point is reached they rebel to some extent and the results will suffer.

People enjoy the status quo and they need to have the feeling that even though changes are required now that eventually their lives will return to that status quo. That means changes will happen, they will become the norm and live will go on from there. If you can instill that kind of feeling people will be receptive to the changes.

But if employees are constantly be confronted with changes all the time they will eventually say "Enough!" and from that point they will resist future changes. The worst possible thing is to introduce a change and then have to make changes to that change again in the future. The more this happens the less confident your employees will become with the program and the management behind it.

Most employees will understand when minor changes are required and sometimes even when major changes are needed. As long as they have faith in management and the company things should be fine.

So if in the past you have been able to make corporate changes easily with few problems your employees will assume that this will continue with the current initiative. But if you had serious problems every time in the past, you should understand if your employees are less than thrilled at what is going to happen now.

From the very start, you should adopt a "do it right the first time" approach to the program, the implementation and the follow-up plans. Everything you do should be done with the idea of doing it once and then move on. This will not only make your employees happy but will also allow you to get things done faster while using less resources.

Overconfidence and Complacency

This is a very real and potentially deadly roadblock when it comes to making changes. Whenever we successfully implement a new philosophy or process in our company or in our lives, there is a profound relief and good feeling when things go well and when we get the benefits or results we were looking for. At that point we feel good about our efforts and all the time, energy and hard work has paid off.

But once that feeling has passed, we sometimes put our efforts aside and start on the next project or the next challenge or problem. We leave the thoughts of customer focus behind and we give all our thoughts and energy to what is happening now. The result of this is that we often forget to circle back every so often to make sure we stay on course and continue our efforts.

This is important for two reasons.

First, our business changes over time as we enter new areas, bring on new products and experience changes in our customer base. Our industry or location experience changes as well with new problems and challenges that might not have existed when we first got started. So the result is that over time we developed new things to address and new challenges that need to be met.

Second, as we change our competition changes as well. Good businesses always watch their competition and when they see another business doing something that makes them better or more efficient, they also look for ways to copy those efforts or improve their business in some other way. So if we remain the same while those around us improve, the net result is that we have taken a step back in comparison.

That is why it is so important that we remain focused on customer service and how our business continues to address and respond to the needs and demands of our customers.

We must understand that what worked yesterday or today might not work nearly as well tomorrow. We also need to understand that what was good enough today might not be nearly good enough tomorrow.

Being customer focused means being pro-active and keeping on top of our business, our industry and our customers. This is NOT a "one and done" type of effort. While we don't have to spend all the time we spent during the creation and implementation phases, we still need to spend some time on follow-up to make sure we stay engaged and focused.

People also tend to become somewhat over confident and unfocused over time as well. So keeping things in focus and circling back with follow-up and refresher training is one way to keep everyone focused on what is best for the customer. Don't get over confident and don't get complacent. If you do you might find yourself and your company falling right back into those old habits.

Striving to be "Good Enough"

Speaking of being good enough, that should NEVER be our end goal. Striving to become "good enough" will keep us from doing our best and performing at our best.

We should never try to rise to the level of customer expectations. Instead, we should strive to always exceed what our customers expect so that we constantly and consistently impress them with the unexpected.

This is important because over time our customers become more demanding and more difficult to impress. What impresses them now will not impress them in the future once your currently level of service becomes commonplace. Because of this we should be constantly looking for ways to get better, ways to improve and to identify anything we can do to make our business more appealing to every customer.

Always look for ways to do anything, no matter how small or apparently trivial for the customer. Remember that what might seem trivial to you might mean a great deal to some customers. It is usually not the big things that impress people but the little things no one really talks about.

So never be satisfied and always look for anything that can be made better. Your business and your customers will love you for it. Your competition, on the other hand, will absolutely hate your guts for it!

How to Get On Top & Stay There!

Ok, now we find ourselves at the point where we have identified our needs, created our program, rolled it out to the employees and are starting to see the results. Business is better, customers are happier and we are beginning to see an increase in sales and customer referrals. At this point we should allow ourselves a few minutes to pat ourselves on the back and congratulate ourselves on a job well done.

But for just a few minutes.

Then we need to take steps to help us rise to the very top and then once we are there, to stay there. This is not as difficult as one might think but there are a few things we need to do now and in the future to help us remain at the top in the future.

Evaluate Your Current Performance

Everything starts with where you are right now. If you are on top, it's good to know that. If you are not quite there, you need to understand what stands between you and getting to the top. That means evaluating every part of your business, or in the case of an individual, your personal performance and career, to see where you need to or can improve.

It is important that you be as critical as you can without being unreasonable. If something is not where it should be, ask questions and don't stop until you receive the answers. Before you can get better you have to know where you are and there is no better time than right now to get started.

Monitor Your Industry and Competition

No matter how much you might not like it, the world doesn't revolve around you and your company. If you are an individual, life does not revolve around you and your skills either. What matters the most is where you stand compared to those businesses and people who are your competition in the marketplace.

If your customer service is great but someone else's is better, then you service isn't that great. You might think so but the reality is that it is not what you think that matters. It is what your customers think that really counts.

Because of this you need to constantly be aware of who your competition is and what they are offering to their customers. If you see anyone doing something better or cheaper than you are doing it, you must take action.

Do not wait for your customers to realize something is better somewhere else. By that time it is too late. Look at your competition NOW and make those changes NOW. Making them after customers leave while being better than nothing still results in your business losing customers and sales.

If the industry in which you do business changes, make every attempt to stay on top of those changes and be one of the leaders and followers. Successful companies rarely play catch-up and when they do they do it quickly. When you are trailing behind anyone else that represents a risk to your business for losing customers and market share. Be a leader and trend setter not a follower.

Look for Any Way to Make Things Even Better

When you are finished changing things, do back and go over everything again to see what can be further improved. Anytime you can do something faster, better or cheaper that is a plus for your customers.

Since a lot of people feel that you don't fix something that isn't broken, looking at things pro-actively can give you a great head start over everyone else!

Just look at some of the advances today when it comes to manufacturing. Products such as computers are getting cheaper and smaller and can store and hold so much more data it is astounding. Imagine if you had stopped trying to improve your products a few years ago when you were at the top. Where do you think you would be today?

Not still at the top, I can assure you of that!

Make it a priority at least once a year to go over every rule, policy and aspect of your business to make sure everything is still the best it can be. Technology and other changes enable people and businesses to accomplish more in less time every day and you need to make sure you remain at the forefront of these changes.

Never be satisfied with where you are. Never think being good enough is good enough. Always look to make things better. Always move forward. Because if everyone else is moving ahead while you stay where you are, you are actually falling further behind and moving backward.

Get Feedback and Use It!

Nothing is better for keeping yourself on top than actually hearing from your employees and your customers. These are the people that really matter to your business. You need responsive and caring employees and you need happy and satisfied customers. If you have both of these you have a winning business. If you have only one of the two, your business is in trouble.

Because customer demands and expectations vary from customer to customer and from year to year, the only people who can guide you and your business are the customers themselves. By going to them direct whether it be by exit poll, survey or direct phone call, you can get exactly what is on their minds.

You will not have to rely on guesswork or conjecture either. You will get actual thoughts and observations by the very people you want to impress and satisfy. This is important because many business base their thoughts and actions based on perceptions of what they feel the customer wants or is feeling.

The problem with perceptions is that they are not always accurate and sometimes they are so far from the truth you would be shocked.

When you base your actions and approaches on false or misleading perception nothing rarely good comes from it. So you want to lose the perceptions and replace them with real data.

Of course, data is only as good as how you actually use it. The best and most comprehensive and accurate data will do you absolutely no good if you get it and place it on a shelf and never open it. In order for data to be useful it has to be analyzed and evaluated and acted upon that is up to management and the people involved in the areas to which the data applies.

Never Be Satisfied

Last, but certainly not least, never be satisfied with where you are or stop trying to better than you are currently doing. Maybe you are doing your best but you should never stop trying. We know we are repeating ourselves when it comes to this topic but it is one of the most important aspects and cornerstones of customer service.

Never stop trying to find ways to make your business easier to deal with. Never stop looking for ways to provide greater value. Most important, never stop looking for ways to show your customers how much you value and appreciate them and how important they are to you and your business.

Create Eager &
Happy Employees

Before we end this book and let you take the information you learned and put it into action, let's talk about one of the most important parts of any customer service program. That part is the employees of your company. If you are an individual reading this book, you are one of the most important parts of the customer experience.

Our employees or individuals are our greatest asset. Though management may feel that they are the driving force behind the company, the day to day customer interaction between the employees and the customers is what takes the company towards success or failure. Employees are the ones who take direction from management and turn it into a customer focused culture. Without those efforts the program would die a slow death.

So it stands to reason that we want to have the best and most well intentioned employees interact with our customers. We want experienced employees who care about the customer and the company they represent. We want people who are going to go through their day taking pride in every success and learning from every mistake or failure.

We also want to establish continuity with our employees as well. We do not want a lot of turnover or for customers to always see new faces when they walk through our doors. We want them to recognize and form a bond between employees they know and have dealt with in the past.

These relationships are what separates quality customer focused businesses from the large and impersonal consumer giants. These are the relationships that enable our business to thrive while others struggle. These are the relationships that keep our customers coming back to us instead of always looking for the lowest price or the most convenient location.

Because of this, it stands to reason that we should make every effort to keep our employees happy and motivated in their jobs. We want them to look at their job as more than just a job. We want them to take pride in what they do and believe in the company that they work for. There are a few ways we can help achieve that goal and none of them require a large amount of resources or time. Yet they will pay huge dividends when it comes to keeping employees happy.

Here are a few ways you can keep your employees happy:

Compensate them Fairly

When all is said and done if people feel that they are grossly underpaid compared to other people in similar positions their attitudes are not going to be the best. While this does not mean that you need to pay your employees more to treat customers better, it is never the less one important factor in how employees feel about the company they work for.

In one company I had worked for they cut employee benefits and bonuses to the core while maintaining and even increasing management incentives and bonuses. The corresponding steep decline in productivity and quality was not a coincidence.

Recognize their Successes

One way to make employees feel better about themselves and more appreciated by the company is to recognize employees when they do good work or experience a success of any kind. This accomplishes two important things.

First, it shows the employee that what they are doing is being noticed by others.

This gives additional meaning to what they do and will give them a reason to keep doing what they are doing.

Second, it makes employees feel appreciated by the company. Just the fact that someone took time to say a nice word or mention their achievement or performance in the company newsletter or announcement often means a great deal to employees. Everyone like to be recognized and praised by others.

Treat them Fairly

Most employees just want to be treated the same as everyone else. Whenever a manager or supervisor treats one or two employees better than everyone else, or treats one group differently, that usually ends badly.

Always make an effort to treat everyone fairly and apply the same rules and factors for evaluating performance on all employees not just a few. This is something that should be easy to do but for some companies and some managers appears quite impossible.

Treat them as People First & Employees Second

Though your employee might wear a badge or a uniform, they are still people first and employees second. That means they want the same things as you and I want and they have the same needs as well.

People go through tough times and have family problems to deal with and employers should be sympathetic in those instances. While this does not mean that an employee is deserving of special treatment, it should mean that an employer should have a heart at times and realize that people need time or to be accommodated in some situations.

Promote from Within

For most people, the opportunity for advancement and the bettering of one's life and career are very important. For that reason, when a company is looking to fill a position they should first look within their current employees to see if there are any who qualify for that position.

While this is not always possible, and while sometimes an outside hire might be needed for a new view or approach to doing business, most of the time hiring and promoting from within will show your employees that their job is more than just a job. It shows that their job can be a career.

If a current employee has all the qualifications need for the job and is deemed a good fit then every effort should be made to offer them the job.

But if they are not qualified, or if others from outside the company have considerably better qualification, then they should not be offered the position. In other words, if they qualify, they should be considered. Nothing more and certainly nothing less.

Do Something Nice for No Reason

A long time ago my manager called me and told me to take my wife out to dinner and expense it to the company. There was no special reason and I had not done anything special or out of the ordinary as the reason for this gesture. It was just something he did for no reason at all as his way of telling me that my contributions to the company were appreciated by him.

I cannot begin to tell you how much I appreciated the gesture. We went out to dinner at a nice place that wasn't all that expensive so the gesture did not cost him a lot. But here we are years later and I still remember it to this day.

Little things like that speak volumes to your employees. Anytime you can do something for your employees for no reason at all, consider it. It might be bringing in pizza for everyone for lunch or handing out movie tickets to the local movie theatre or just about anything just to show your appreciation. You will probably bet many times you investment back in good will and increased productivity.

Listen to Them

Here is one of the easiest and least expensive ways of making an employee feel appreciated.

Just listen to them. If they have a thought or a comment, listen to them. If they have an idea or suggestions, listen to them. If they have a solution to a problem, then consider implementing it. All people really want from their boss, manager or supervisor is to be listened to.

When you ignore someone or fail to make an effort to listen to them you are actually telling them that what they have to say could not possibly be worth the time you would spend on listening to them. That is not something you want to convey to anyone in life, employees included. So take your time and listen to what your employees have to say. Take it one step further and solicit their opinions and comments a couple of times a year. Make them feel like they are a valued piece of the company.

And all you need to do to accomplish that is listen to them once in a while. Surely you have time for that!

Conclusion

There was a lot of information in this book and we hope you found it interesting and valuable to you. We also hope it has given you a few ideas and has enabled you to know how to get started and where to take things from there.

The fact that you purchased this book and have read it through to this point speaks volumes about you as a person and as part of a company. It shows that you have a clear desire to make things better and it shows that you understand the value of establishing a great relationship with your customers. There are many reasons for believing this and moving forward. But regardless of your reasons there is one thing that will always remain true when it comes to making any type of change.

You can only create a change by doing something!

If you think you can make anything change without changing anything, you are in for a rude awakening. If you change nothing, nothing will change. If you fail to take action, you will fail to make any changes in your life, your career and in your company.

So now it is up to you. We have given you a lot of information and a lot to think about. In other words, we have given you a set of tools to start you on your way. But if you never take action, if you never open up your toolbox and use some of the tools we gave you, nothing will happen.

So what you need to do now is perhaps the hardest part of all. You need to take that first step and start things rolling. You don't have to make massive changes or take a massive first step. The size of the step is not as important as just taking it. Don't be afraid of what might happen. Be afraid of what won't happen if you stay where you are!

Everyone who has read this book is capable of creating great changes and accomplishing great things. But whether you want to change a rule or change the world, every change starts with a single step. Soo all you have to do now is take that first step. Not tomorrow or next week or next year. Take it now and then watch things happen.

Go ahead, take it.

Take it now.

For more books and
information on customer
service training, please visit
our website at:

http://www.infowhse.com

www.ingramcontent.com/pod-product-compliance
Lightning Source LLC
Chambersburg PA
CBHW051856170526
45168CB00001B/133